To Iraq & Back
On War & Writing

To Iraq & Back
On War & Writing

by

Jessica Scott

Portions of this book originally appeared on www.jessicascott.net online.

ISBN: 978-1942102007

Cover design courtesy of Shawntelle Madison

For more information please see www.jessicascott.net

A **free** eBook edition is available
with the purchase of this print book.

CLEARLY PRINT YOUR NAME ABOVE IN UPPER CASE

Instructions to claim your free eBook edition:
1. Download the BitLit app for Android or iOS
2. Write your name in **UPPER CASE** on the line
3. Use the BitLit app to submit a photo
4. Download your eBook to any device

Contents

Foreword

This is my blog. There are many like it, but this is mine.

I wrote this blog while I served in Mosul, Iraq in 2009.

It was my first deployment.

It was my second time away from my children in their short lives.

It was my first duty station as an officer instead of an enlisted soldier.

It was a formative experience and it shaped me in ways I'm still understanding.

I wrote because it gave me an outlet from the chaos, the calm, and the frustration. I wrote because I thought people might be interested in what life was like for a REMF.

The book you're about to read does not include commentary on the posts though it has been edited for clarity; it is merely the posts captured and put into a single format to make it easier to read.

This blog is mine: my views here should not be taken to represent any official policy or commentary on the DOD, the Army, or any other entity. They are solely mine.

This is just part of my journey as a writer, as a mom, as a soldier, as a wife heading to combat for the first time.

For those of you who are reading it for the first time, thank you for picking it up.

For those of you who have read it from the beginning and are rereading it, thank you for sharing it with me all over again.

Predeployment
2008

Hello, World!
October 18, 2008

THERE WON'T BE MUCH traffic here until mid-to-late December, but I'll post a little before I go. Once we get settled across the pond, check back daily! Of course, there will be NO OPSEC violations on this blog. I won't share anything that will risk any soldier's life. Mostly, it will be my observations and experiences as I go through my combat tour with the First Cav.

Later,

Jess

Food Battles
October 31, 2008

SO I'M A FEW weeks out from deploying to Iraq. Guess how I choose to spend my last few weeks with my kids? Fighting about food. We're on day four of my eldest's hunger strike. She has to eat at least one bite of the food we put in front of her or she doesn't eat.

She's opted not to eat. The thing is, she's so stubborn. I honestly think I might lose this battle, but I'm afraid if I cave in now that I've started, it will be over for the rest of her life.

Anyone got any tips? I'd love to break this stalemate and get back to enjoying our time together. My biggest worry is that I'll die in Iraq and my daughter will remember me as the evil

1

mommy who tried to make her eat pizza (yes, the child won't even eat pizza!).

Suggestions welcome!

Surrender
November 7, 2008

SO, I'M A SUCKY parent, but I gave in. Something about fighting a never-ending battle for the last two weeks I'm going to spend with my child for over a year made me reconsider just how much I wanted her to eat green beans. I decided not that much. So, we've taken a new track. I cook. If she eats, great. If not, oh well. I'm just not cooking anything else. So we're at an impasse, so to speak. But as the clock winds down to the day I say goodbye to my babies, I'll look on this as a good decision. Who wants to spend the small amount of time fighting? I'd rather bake pies and have a good time at the zoo.

Later,

Jess

What I'm Reading Now
November 11, 2008

SO I'M HAVING AN apocalyptic bent. I'm reading The Stand by Stephen King. The unabridged version on my new toy, my iPod Touch. I started The Stand several years ago (it may even have been a decade ago) but for some reason I never finished it. I'm glad I didn't then, because I'm enjoying the ride oh so much. The best part about The Stand is that I don't know how it ends, other than most everyone gets sick from the Army-engineered flu.

And as I get ready to head into theater, I'm finding latent interest in religion resurrecting. I'm feeling my own version of an apocalyptic story starting to germinate in my brain, so we'll see what my year in Iraq brings.

The other book my husband recommends is Swan Song. Anyone want to learn something neat? I'm willing to bet that Stephenie Meyer pays tribute to Swan Song and The Stand in her Twilight series. I could be wrong, but her main characters' last names are Swan and Cullen. Coincidence? Or just cool.

One thing the Army teaches us is to honor those that came before us, so if she is paying tribute to those authors, bravo!

So today, on Veteran's Day, let's pause to honor those who gave the ultimate sacrifice and those who haven't, but who give up something of their lives so the rest of the nation can go about their daily business without worrying over who is going to protect them from the boogeyman.

That's all for now.

Jess

A Huge Thank You
November 12, 2008

FOR THOSE OF YOU who don't know, I'm a member of the Austin Romance Writers of America.

They've been amazingly supportive over the ups and downs of going through the pain of seeking publication and last night was no exception.

They threw me a going away party, complete with an Inject the Venom cake and a song. I'm going to say I've never heard a more beautiful rendition of "God Bless America" than the one Lexi Connor sang last night. It moved me to tears. The cards and notes are going with me, so when the bad days come next year, I'll have some cheerful thoughts to remind me. The cake was donated by Cake Please and was amazing!

Folks, if you ever have a chance to swing by a meeting at the RWA in Austin, you really should. You'll leave a better person for knowing them.

And before I forget, HUGE congratulations to Skylar White on her publication offer. It was a great way to end the evening. Celebrate, girl!

Okay, that's all.

I'm a Mac
November 13, 2008

SO, I'M WORKING ON finishing up my total migration over to Mac from my PC. I have to say, I'm nervous, primarily because I know how to find data on my hard drive if my Windows craps out. I've heard, though I have not verified, that if you lose your data on a Mac it's gone for good. Thank Steve Jobs for Time Machine. So we'll see. The only thing I'm having trouble with is my Quicken. My PC

Quicken files are not compatible with my Mac Quicken. I've found a work around for the Outlook to Entourage thing.

Oh, and one more little gadget I'm in love with: my iPod Touch. You heard me rave about the little sucker regarding the ebook reader. Well, I can also check my email, balance my checkbook, and so much more. The more I use it, the more I love it. It's the iPhone without the phone (which probably wouldn't work in Iraq anyway).

So that's all for now!

Jess

It's That Time
November 15, 2008

SO THE SECOND WEEK in November is done and gone. Why is that anything to remark on? My family and I are down to our last two weeks together as a family for at least a year. It sucks but it's the life we've chosen as part of the Army. So if anyone has any suggestions for dealing with crushing depression and missing of one's children during my upcoming deployment, I'd love to hear it.

Later!

On the Road Again
November 18, 2008

SO MY FAMILY AND I are somewhere outside Knoxville, getting ready to cut across North Carolina on the way to MomMom and PopPop's house up in Delaware on the first stop in the journey to drop the kids and all the pets off for the year.

I have to say, this has been the most relaxing trip we've taken so far. The kids have been angels and even the psycho cat hasn't been that annoying and I cannot honestly recall when I've been this patient. It sucks that I can't be like this all the time... Anyway, I'm keeping my mind busy and trying not to think about next Friday (The Departure) when the year away from the kids and pets and home officially begins. I'm trying to figure out how to post the donut of despair up on my website, so you all can count down with me. Otherwise, I'm just ready to get started so I can get it over with already.

That's all for now!

A Good Day
November 23, 2008

IT'S NOT OFTEN THAT extreme amounts of manual labor result in a good day, but today was it. My kids got to spend it with their entire family on my husband's side as we did some remodeling at my in-law's house. It was great and a day my oldest will remember for a long time as her uncle let her help drive the Bobcat. I have pictures. It was great. But the best part was that my kids got to spend time with their MomMom and PopPop, something they don't get nearly enough time doing. Now mind you, MomMom hooked them up with marshmallows so she's forever in their good graces, but it was a really great day for memories. And after all, isn't that what today is for? Making memories...

So here's the thing. Take a minute out of your day and hug your kids. Even when you want to smother them, give 'em a quick squeeze. Make that the memory they remember, instead of fighting over eating pizza. Cause you might not get the chance tomorrow to make a better one.

That's all for now!

Jess

Home for a Minute
November 30, 2008

SO THE LEAVING IS over, at least for now. Nothing can describe the feeling of having your four year old look at you and ask why you're sad and then having to explain that you'll be gone for a while. But she's a smart kid. She said, "But you'll have Daddy with you, right? And Daddy makes you happy?" Not as happy as being around my kids, but yeah, having Daddy around will help.

I'm not going to complain, because others have done this way more than I have. I'm going to be grateful. Grateful that we have my mom to take care of our kids. Grateful that they're healthy and overall happy. And grateful for the time that I have had with them. And I won't mope (okay, not too much) because my kids love being with my mom.

So. I'm not going to complain about how bad this sucks, I'm going to be grateful for the opportunities ahead and pray that everyone comes home safe this year.

That's all for now.

Jess

Oovoo, My Friend
December 2, 2008

SO, I'VE DISCOVERED A handy little thing to help me keep in touch with the kids. Oovoo. It's video teleconferencing via the web and it's FREE.

The big plus was that it only takes two steps for my computer-illiterate (I mean that in the nicest way, Mom) mom to dial us, plus she already figured out how to leave us video messages. Pretty cool. Still working some bandwidth issues, but hey, anything

Jessica Scott

that lets me see my kids while I'm deployed is worth it.

That said, I've been slacking off on my To Do list. I've got a ton of stuff to accomplish and yeah, I'm waiting until the last minute to do it. Like finish medical readiness. Wills. You know, the important things. Got to get cracking.

Oh and in the keep-myself-busy department: I accomplished 5000 words today in my latest WIP, Saving Trent. Not bad in the way of occupied so I don't sit around and miss the kiddies. I'm hoping to have this book done before the new year.

That's all for now!

Jess

The Packing Is Done
December 6, 2008

SO TOMORROW IS THE big day. I'm off, the packing is done for the most part (okay eighty percent but pretty dang close) and all that's left to do is get up and go.

And I won't say that I'm not nervous. This isn't a training exercise; it's real. I can only hope that at the end of the day, I don't do something that gets someone hurt or worse. I'm grateful that my husband is going with me. I'm grateful my mom is taking great care of my kids. And I'm grateful that I have a huge long wait tomorrow to do nothing but sit around and wait to get on a plane (and hope my duffle bag fits).

So if you're interested, drop me a line sometime this year. I'd love to hear from you.

Let the adventure begin.

See you whenever I get internet access again! Check back soon, as I have no idea when that may be. :)

Jess

Made It!
December 8, 2008

MADE IT SAFE AND sound to Kuwait. Did a little work today, but the major grind starts tomorrow. Pretty jet lagged but can't seem to get used to sleeping. It's just like being at NTC (the National Training Center at Fort Irwin), as far as the sand and the five-minute combat showers, so all in all, it's not bad.

Except that I didn't do any writing on the plane. Nothing. Not a single word. I slept instead, which may explain my current insomnia. I'd like to write something but I'm just not feeling into it. Though I did discover a cool fact during a layover: Stanza (eReader app for iPod and iPhone) offers many classics for FREE. I downloaded Poe, Hawthorne, Neitzsche. All kinds of good stuff.

That's all the excitement for now! Otherwise, I'm on Day 1. 364 to go.

Task and Purpose, People
December 11, 2008

OKAY, I RECOGNIZE THAT leadership is not an inherited trait. Some people are better at it than others. But some people have no business being leaders. They should really get out of the Army and go home because they do a disservice to soldiers in the Army. They should also realize that they need to stay in their functional areas of expertise and not tell other people's soldiers what to do.

And on the flip side of that, I am NOT a noncommissioned officer any more. I am a lieutenant and that means when a captain, regardless of how experienced, tells me to do something, I have to do it. Even when I KNOW I have a different mission. But that's okay. That's how the Army works and it works that way for a reason. Lieutenants do what captains tell them. Let's just leave it at that, for now. I'm going to finish my book.

Later,

Jess

Let's Talk About the S-word
December 12, 2008

NO, NOT THAT S-WORD. Stress. Too many folks over here are already starting to show signs of breaking down. It's Day 5. One thing I've learned from my husband's two previous tours over here is that a year in Iraq is a marathon, not a sprint. If you don't get enough rest, if you don't eat right, the stress is going to get you way before anything else.

Stress over here comes in many forms. Missing your family is stressful. People may not acknowledge that it is, but a lack of little kids' feet slapping on bare floors is stressful. Life with kids has a certain sound. Life in the tents over here has a different sound, one of air conditioners and national anthems. People are used to hearing certain sounds when they sleep, so listening to shouts and a/c units causes stress.

The biggest thing I can recommend is for you to find a way to deal with the stress. An outlet that lets you channel the energy the stress is taking out of you and put it toward something that makes the unit better.

So that's all for now.

Later!

1 Week Down, 51 To Go
December 14, 2008

SO THE FIRST WEEK has given new meaning to the phrase Hurry Up and Wait. Troops are arriving and training is underway. All in all, I give the training camp here in Kuwait a thumbs up so far. They have a lot of soldiers to deal with here and they're only here for a few weeks before heading north. The USO is cool. They have a small studio set up so you can read stories to your kids on video camera and then send them the DVD and the book. It's really great.

Otherwise, the drama continues as people continue to be stressed out by the things going on here. I wonder what's going to happen when we go north. I also wonder how I'm going to handle things and my biggest worry is that I'll do something stupid to get someone else hurt. I try very hard not to pull rank and I really listen when people with experience over here talk, especially people who've had combat experience.

I've already learned one lesson: always be ready. People kind of snickered when the CSM (command sergeant major) said to make sure you're ready for a fight when you ride off base. I had my first opportunity to go off base here in Kuwait yesterday and the trip was enlightening.

I'll go in to more detail some other time, but let's just say I didn't sleep the entire trip. It was too interesting and I didn't want to miss anything. Culture Shock Part 1 coming next.

My Muse is On Strike
December 15, 2008

SO I WAS GOING for the gold with Saving Trent. I was on a roll. On the flight back to Texas after dropping off my kids, I wrote 5000 words and was on track to keep right on going until the end.

And now? Nothing. Okay, not really nothing. I've written about eight hundred words this week, when I should be doing a thousand per day. I think I'm going to have to declare publicly that I will write a thousand words per day in order to get my butt back in front of the computer.

I think part of my problem is the new environment: it's austere and boring and there are no outside distractions. I have nothing to force me to sit and write.

So I think I've come up with a solution. However, it involves more than just a thousand words per day. I edited my playlists and I've got new music to listen to that's getting my brain moving again. But the biggest thing is that I owe it to my characters to finish this book. I just can't leave them hanging in the void left on the blank pages.

My goal is therefore declared: finish Saving Trent. I will write a thousand words per day, every day, until it is finished. I will not allow my characters to end where they sit right now (one is home with three very upset children and one is getting a much needed girls day out).

Besides that, I'm afraid that if I don't start writing again, it will just slip to the side and I'll be one of those writers who gave up. What am I talking about? I don't quit.

So there. Off my butt, time to stop blogging and get on with it. And that's what's going on in my world today!

A Fun Escape
December 19, 2008

SO, THE OTHER DAY in my shop we were scrounging for a power cable to a VoiP phone (don't ask). We managed to find one down at Arifjan, a several hour drive away. I told the boss that my husband was heading to Ali Al Saleem and I could ask him if he could scoot a little further down the road to AJ. Well, it turns out that my husband needed another person in his vehicle anyway so off we went.

What a fun day. It was by far the most relaxing day we've had here. We saw a bunch of camels on the side of the road at feeding time. They're actually pretty cool to look at, not at all like that a-hole camel out at Topsey in Copperas Cove (for those of you who don't know, that camel sticks his head in the car and steals the food you've bought to feed all the animals). It was a lot of fun seeing them and we were wondering what purpose exactly do camels serve out here. Hubby said they were a status symbol, kind of like an Escalade in the States.

Oh well, the adventure continues. Muse is back in performing shape. Apparently all I have to do to get her back to work is complain about her and she gets creative on me.

So now I'm off to work at exciting Camp Buehring, Kuwait. That's all for now!

Jess

Merry Christmas, Welcome To Iraq
December 24, 2008

WELL, WE'RE HERE. I'M sharing a CHU (containerized housing unit) with my husband, there're hot showers and real toilets. What else could a girl want in a combat zone? No internet, however, so blog posts will be somewhat more sporadic for a few weeks until we get situated. Otherwise, we're here, it's Christmas and at least I'm with my husband.

Kiss your kids goodnight and remember how fortunate you are to be home with them right now.

Merry Christmas, everyone.

Jessica Scott

Deployment
2009

It's a New Year!

January 2, 2009

IN CASE YOU WERE wondering, internet access is sporadic and will continue to be for the next couple of weeks until we get settled in.

All in all, things are going well. If you feel like sending anything, send coffee and Coffeemate, all different flavors. The Army runs on coffee, some more than others.

I'll post more later, once things settle down about life, mud, and things overall in Iraq.

Take care!

What's in My Pockets

January 3, 2009

LAURA GRIFFIN ONCE ASKED me what I carried in my uniform pockets and I've been updating her periodically, but I thought the rest of you might be interested in what I lug around every day.

First, my M4 goes with me everywhere, except to shower in the morning. I have a bad habit of setting things down, so I wear it over my shoulder almost all the time. I usually only set it down when I'm going to be at my desk for a minute (not often right now). Around my belt, I wear a Surefire flashlight and a Leatherman multitool (which has a knife). In my cargo pockets, I have my green notebook that also doesn't get set down (it goes in my pocket, otherwise I'd set it down and walk off and spend half the day looking for it). In my other cargo pocket, I carry a kabuki brush (to knock the dust off my weapon and computers), as well as baby wipes. When they're not being worn, I have my gloves, eye protection glasses and my patrol cap in that pocket as well.

I have pens in one shoulder pocket, and a couple of markers, as well as a laser pointer (the hallmark of a good lieutenant, according to the Signal schoolhouse:). In another pocket, I carry my iPod, because the only way to get any work done is to plug in and ignore the world around you (plus it has my ebooks on it. I just finished the Twilight series—thoughts on that later). Another pocket contains my wallet, which I also put right back.

In one lower leg pocket, I carry a 30 round magazine (the rest of my basic load of ammo is on my IBA (body armor)) and in my other leg pocket I carry a reflective belt and a headlamp (it gets really, really dark at night here).

So that's what's in my pockets on a daily basis. I figure my pants probably weigh about ten pounds. Good times, huh? But hey, a girl's got to be prepared.

What Keeps Me Busy
January 6, 2009

3

SO BY NOW EVERYONE has heard on the news and in the paper about units replacing other units, but what really happens? Here's an OPSEC (operational security) approved RIP/TOA (relief in place/transfer of authority) brief.

RIP: Relief in Place. What it really means is the outgoing unit pulls out bits and pieces once ours are up and running and ready to step in.

TOA: Transfer of Authority. The outgoing commander controls the battle-space until this date when the new commander assumes responsibility.

So how does this influence the Signal world, which I'm a part of?

Well, for starters, each brigade has its own organic servers and other equipment that allows us to communicate. So the incoming brigade has to put its equipment in the same place and get it stood up so the outgoing unit can leave. It should be a relatively simple process, but like everything in the Army, no plan survives first contact. Equipment is broken, parts are missing, it's a never-ending process of holy crap this isn't going to work. Eventually, everything falls into place one way or another but long days and competent operators help tremendously.

We also have to transfer phone numbers and computers from their servers to ours and ensure that the outgoing commander still has the ability to command and control his battle-space.

It's been a huge learning experience so far and digital RIP is still several days off.

The TOA is a physical transfer, much like a change of command. It symbolizes the outgoing commander's transfer of responsibility for the soldiers on the ground to the incoming commander.

Speaking of commanders, my brigade commander, COL Gary Volesky and his CSM James Pippin have some interesting history, if anyone is interested. COL Volesky was involved in the first big fight for Sadr City in '04 and CSM Pippin is legendary in his own right (allegedly instead of running from an ambush, he directed his driver to head for the shooter). You can read about the Sadr City battle in Martha Raddatz' book The Long Road Home. It gives a great perspective on how this commander views his responsibilities as a leader of soldiers.

Anyway, that's all for now!

Take care.

1 Month Down
January 11, 2009

SO I'VE OFFICIALLY BEEN gone for a little over a month now and I've learned a couple of pretty important lessons.

One: no one is irreplaceable. I've said before that Jesus Himself could command the First Cavalry Division but the day would come when He would change command. I have to keep reminding myself of that and also instilling that in my soldiers. I have one guy who works his ass off but hates sharing information because he feels like it will make him less valuable to the team. He's getting better though, under the guidance of our outstanding new Automations NCOIC (you know the kind of sergeant who is not only technically proficient but also a solid leader: a new lieutenant's wish come true).

Two: prioritize. Everyone over here thinks their mission is important and we are all part of the team that helps the commander make informed decisions but some folks are unwilling to work with the system that we have. They want their own SIPR drops (classified network) as opposed to just logging on to someone else's computer. These folks tend to get pretty upset when you tell them they have to wait. And it is so much fun being a lieutenant telling a major sir, you're not a priority right now. That always works out so well for me.

Three: no one is exempt from guard duty. I was pretty upset the other day when in the middle of digital RIP, every one of my soldiers was taken from the helpdesk either for guard duty or detail or something else that at the time was way less important than what we were doing. However, the mission continued (though I did walk away for a few minutes to avoid losing my temper) and overall, the digital RIP has gone much better than expected.

Four: this year is a marathon, not a sprint. This may turn out to be my most important lesson yet. When faced with eating an elephant, you can only take one bite at a time. Slow down and plug away at it. You'll get there.

So one month is already gone and it's gone by pretty quickly. I only hope the rest of the year goes as quickly and I'll be home with my kids before I know it.

Take care!

Feeling Unsettled
January 15, 2009

I DON'T PANIC. NOT in an our-base-is-being-bombed kind of way. I just feel...edgy. Like I need to be doing something more than I am. Or like maybe I'm waiting for the other shoe to drop.

So let's talk about this writing thing I keep doing. I've spent a huge chunk of time over the last two years learning, reading, and writing, working on this project or that and somehow I feel like I'm standing in the same place that I was last year at this time, when I received my first ever agent request (that was a heady feeling, let me tell you). Since then, I've gotten some great rejections and lots of helpful comments and yet, I continue to work on that next book.

Over here in Iraq, I find myself watching how people look, how they carry themselves, because here is the heart of the stories I tell. How people are impacted by being over here. It dawned on me (and there's no way for this not to come off condescending, because I'm here with my husband, but that is not how this comment is meant) that it is incredibly lonely over here. For folks who have been here before, the loneliness is something they're used to, something to be dealt with by meet-ups at chow or at the gym. But I don't think anyone can truly grasp the aloneness that soldiers feel being away from everything that is familiar and comforting and...home until you're actually here.

So as I watch people adjust to these conditions, I realize I'm learning about myself, too. How am I adjusting and changing because of my experiences over here? (Which have been incredibly mundane, so don't worry, Mom.) We'll have to see how this changes my writing.

Take care!

Jess

Rule Number 2
January 18, 2009

I JUST FINISHED READING Heidi Squire Kraft's book Rule Number 2. You can find it at Amazon or BN.com, if you're interested. Even though this is my first deployment and it is in no way the same as Dr Kraft's deployment near Fallujah, I can relate to a couple of things she wrote about.

First, and probably the most humorous, is the Legend of the Camel Spider. Not only do I live in absolute terror of ever stumbling across this thing, but her chapters about the legend of it are absolutely true. You'd think these things could get as big as a dog from the way soldiers talk about them. One soldier in the S2 (intel shop) spoke about being chased by one last deployment. Needless to say, I'm not looking forward to seeing one and I'm pretty sure my husband is going to go out of his way to show me one at the first opportunity.

The second part I really relate to: Dr Kraft talks about disconnecting from her family, from her kids. She writes about not crying about them and being unable to be both mom and deployed soldier (my term not hers). She had to make a choice and for the time she spent in the war zone, she chose to focus on being a wartime doc. When she got home, she had trouble reconnecting with her patients and with her family.

I have to say, even though my homecoming is a long way off, I worry about reconnecting with my kids. I'm also worried about how being over here in this environment is going to change my relationship with my husband. Things aren't business as usual over here, no matter how much I might wish them to be or might joke about them being just that.

Things change, people change, and war changes people a lot. Dr Kraft's book takes one woman's journey through a pretty horrible time during this war and brings her home again. Most of us won't go through what she went through; many of us will go through something worse. We'll just have to see what the outcome is for each of us, as individuals, don't you think?

Name that Book
January 19, 2009

I ABSOLUTELY HATE THE title of my book, Saving Trent. HATE IT. So, I'm opening up the bidding for suggestions. You don't win anything super cool but you'll have my eternal gratitude.

So here's the blurb/summary: Laura Davilla loves her husband but the war has kept him from her for four long years. When she learns that he's been volunteering for deployments to stay away from his family, Laura's had enough. The threat of losing his wife is enough to force Trent home, but is Laura's love enough to save him from the nightmares he's spent four years running from?

That's the teaser. I'd love some suggestions for a title. Post them here or email them to me. I really want something classy yet serious.

Thanks!

Help For Kids
January 20, 2009

AS MOST OF YOU know by now, I'm stationed in Mosul, Iraq and we've got an education problem (like most of the Middle East). See, there are schools over here and some of them have like eight hundred kids, four teachers, and ten books (this is a number from an actual school and I'm sure these numbers are reflected across our footprint). Anyway, I'm asking for help.

Can you round up pencils, crayons, and kids books (text books, ABCs, counting books, coloring books, anything at all) (not sure if you can find any in Arabic but that would help tremendously, too, as the literacy rate is abysmal).

The only way we have a chance in changing the hearts and minds in this region is through education and showing the children that there is a better way. I figure we can start small with coloring books of kids playing instead of throwing rocks, you know?

Soccer balls, stuffed animals, all of that sort of thing would be greatly appreciated. So can you all pool together and ship as much of those types of things as you can?

Anything you can do to help is greatly appreciated! Thank you for your support!

Thank you!
January 23, 2009

A SINCERE THANK YOU to everyone who has responded to the call for school supplies. I've had an overwhelming number of people and several chapters of the RWA (Austin RWA, CTRWA, Montana and Oklahoma RWA chapters, you all rock!) pledge their support, as well as fellow RomVet members and folks off the Clues and News Loop from the RWA Kiss of Death chapter.

I can't thank all of you enough for your support, not only of me and my soldiers while we're over here, but for the Iraqi people as well.

Thank you for being willing to get involved and make a difference in the lives of Iraqi kids. It means so much to all of us over here.

Take care.

It's Finished
January 24, 2009

YAY! I FINISHED MY fourth book, once titled Saving Trent. Thanks to the input I received I'm going with All That Remains as a title.

So now, the book is off to the fabulous and brutal critique partner for a shredding, then it's edit time for me and the query process begins again. Woohoo.

In the meantime, I've still got that pesky writing challenge from the Austin RWA, where I have to write every day for a month and dang it, the month is only half over. So I've got to come up with the next one. I'll let you know what I come up with!

That's all for now!

A New Book
January 28, 2009

SO YOU'RE PROBABLY WONDERING what I've been up to the last couple of days. I buried myself in a new project, having finished the first draft of All That Remains (the novel formerly known as Saving Trent).

The new book is tentatively titled The Last Sunrise and I'm indulging my religious side a little. For those of you that know me, you know that studying religion has been a particular hobby of mine for a very, very long time (I earned my BA in religious studies). This book explores what happens if a man is the driving force toward bringing about the apocalypse instead of some divine plan.

Oh and my very first book, After the War, the book I keep putting under the bed that keeps resurrecting itself, has taken third in the Silicone Valley RWA's Gotcha Contest. Another Austin RWA member Lexi Connor took second with her manuscript Dance Away Danger. Congrats, Lexi!

It was a great contest with some great feedback for my novel.

Take care!

A New Job
January 31, 2009

WELL, IT'S OFFICIAL. ON Monday, I move from the brigade staff down to a platoon leader position. For those of you that aren't familiar with the rank structure, I'm going to move from being in charge of no one and only responsible for planning communications, to being responsible for a platoon of soldiers. I'm getting a really good platoon sergeant, which is good, and I've got a good group of soldiers that I'm falling in on.

So, in the grand scheme of things, what does that mean? It means I go from planning the mission to making the mission happen. It will be good. I'll get to actually experience the relationship between a platoon sergeant and a platoon leader from the platoon leader side of it (I've been a platoon sergeant before in my past life as an E7 Sergeant First Class). And I get to get back to what's really important, taking care of soldiers. I've got a bunch of young talent and that's exciting.

So that's all for now!

Thank You for the Supplies
February 1, 2009

I JUST RECEIVED A box of pencils and crayons from Student Supply in Kent, Washington. There wasn't any way for me to identify who sent the box, but I wanted to say thank you to whoever sent it. I'm passing them along to the company commanders and wanted to pass along my thanks to the Secret Santa!

I can't thank you enough for your support.

Jess

Initiation
February 4, 2009

WOW, I HAVE A new appreciation for pain. I was fully initiated into my new company today.

They laid me on a table and stuck a breathing tube down my nose. You have to get the full visual: the tube is six inches long and a good quarter inch around. They lube it up, pull your nose back and start feeding that sucker in and oh by the way, it has to puncture the membrane in the back of your nose before it can get all the way down your throat. I think my sinuses are still bleeding.

Now before you wonder why this torture, consider that it is a lifesaving skill when a soldier's face has been damaged enough to prevent them from breathing.

I have to get the pictures from my First Sergeant but I have been officially initiated!

A Rare Comment on Policy
February 11, 2009

FIRST, WELCOME BACK. THE blog took a hit for a few days last week because of network issues but I'm back now, for the time being.

Anyway, an issue from this war hit up close and personal this week. Since President Bush 41, photographing the caskets of our fallen brothers and sisters has been banned. I saw today that this policy is being reexamined. While I will fully support and carry out the orders of those appointed over me, I sincerely hope this administration will leave the ban in place.

It is not because of any desire to hide the cost of this war in lives. It is not to protect anyone's right to privacy because there is no way to identify who is carried in which casket. The entire reason I want this ban to remain in place is to honor our brothers and sisters and carry out the process of their return home with quiet dignity and respect.

While I can understand that most reporters and photographers would conduct themselves and treat the results of their work in a respectful manner, inevitably there would be that one who would desecrate the photos or use them as part of a protest. Our soldiers gave their lives to protect and defend the Constitution, and yes, that involves free speech even to the point of disrespecting our fallen brothers and sisters. That, however, does not make the thought any less distasteful or disgusting to me as a soldier or as an American.

We owe it to our brothers and sisters who have made the ultimate sacrifice to respect the last honors this nation bestows on them and not to create a public spectacle of their final return home. People who wish to protest or advertise the cost of this war should find another way to do so and remember that human decency should impact their decisions. People who wish to pay their respects should find another way as well, preferably one that involves permission from the families.

But please, leave the honors due to our fallen brothers and sisters where they belong: with the families and friends of the fallen. We as a nation owe it to the families to respect them, as well as their fallen loved ones.

Yay Me
February 15, 2009

OKAY, IT'S NOT OFTEN this happens, but I'm going to skip to work tomorrow. I'm getting promoted. Now don't get too excited. The promotion from Second Lieutenant to First Lieutenant is usually as automatic as from Private to Private First Class. But I'll finally get to color that gold bar black (I've actually been threatened with a serious amount of pushups if I color in my rank).

I'll probably only get promoted once more in the Army, so I'm going to enjoy my day, God willing. My husband is here with me and he'll get to promote me. And it will only be the second promotion in our Army careers that my husband has gotten to promote me. My daughters pinned on my 2LT bars after OCS (officer candidate school) in 2007.

So have a beer for me and celebrate for me. I'll have a beer next year when my brigade comes home.

Take care!

Need to Appreciate Feeling Like a Girl
February 17, 2009

OKAY, I'VE ALWAYS WALKED a fine line between tomboy and girlie girl. But this is getting ridiculous. I actually broke out mascara and eyeliner yesterday for my promotion (hey, it was a special day that I figured deserved a little makeup;

plus, there were pictures involved). So anyway, my husband, bless his heart, makes the comment that, yeah, I look better with a little makeup than without.

I love the man dearly but, seriously. Really? So my wicked side is coming out and I'm thinking I can go really overboard and put the eyeliner on like skank black and line the eye, the inner eye, and draw a cat tail. That would get some looks, don't you think? I thought it was funny more than anything because I really only put on a touch of it. Just enough to feel like a girl again.

I'm probably going to go off the deep end. Someone call Lauren at the Bobbi Brown counter at Saks in Austin. Mama's coming home in about a year and we're going to have us a session. (And my husband is having kittens at this very moment at the thought of me loose in Saks at the makeup counters.) I've gotten much better with age and the funny thing about being over here: I don't have the slightest urge to shop. I think it's got something to do with everyone wearing the same thing. There's no competition, no sizing up this girl's purse or that girl's shoes. It's kind of liberating in a way, so I can kind of understand where feminists say that removing all the material things makes us more conscious of who we are, not what we have.

So another lesson learned from life in Iraq. Let's see how it translates when I get back to real life in the States.

Women at War
February 21, 2009

I'VE BEEN DEBATING ABOUT posting regarding an issue I've been dealing with over here, but I decided to share my severely edited thoughts with the world. I'm a strong proponent of women being able to do what they are capable of, with their own limitations being the only discriminator. That means doing their job as soldiers just like everyone else, right? Now I'm not a fan of women in combat arms as a rule, but that's another discussion for another time. A non-direct action job shouldn't be an issue, right?

Here's the situation. My platoon is responsible for occupying a radio relay site. They are remotely located from here. There are showers and latrines and a single sleeping area. Two different units are responsible for the two different sites. On the western site, the occupying unit will not allow females on their site because they say the living conditions are too harsh and there was a rape at one of these sites during the last unit's rotation. And that really pisses me off and yet, I don't get a vote. But the short version is we have females who are not allowed to do their jobs right now at a certain site because of something that happened to the last unit on the last deployment.

I'd love to hear differing opinions on this. The soldiers would be pulling shifts monitoring the communications equipment. Should I argue that the females go out to both sites or just let it lie?

A Sacrifice of Chocolate
February 24, 2009

MOST OF YOU WHO know me know that I have two pretty big vices (there are more, but these are the major ones): chocolate and swearing. So, for Lent, this year, I'm going to give up both. Yes, I know, these things have not worked for me in the past. But I'm not giving up sugar, I'm giving up chocolate. So supreme stress will still be fed. I'm lucky, as my muse is addicted to music, not chocolate. I'd probably go insane over here if I wasn't writing, so it's a good thing my goals aren't going to be counterproductive.

Anyway, as for the swearing, I think my brain is hardwired to swear. It's like a bad habit that's full grown into the muscle memory of how I talk and react. So we'll see if I can rewire the profanity section of my head. It's not going to count, however, if I put a curse word into my writing. Once again, need to feed the muse and she's demanding that I put what really happens onto the paper, not the ideal.

So. That's my goal for the next forty days, she says, sitting here eating dark chocolate M&Ms (thanks Al!). Wish me luck.

I'm going to need it.

The Last Sunrise is DONE
February 26, 2009

OKAY, SO I'M GOING to share my little thrill that The Last Sunrise is finished and now safely tucked away while I figure out the next book. That book was exhausting to write. I poured out 97,700 words in about thirty days (thank you Austin Romance Writers of America writing challenge). The story grabbed hold of me and didn't let go. I did struggle a few times getting through it and I KNOW it's a first draft, but it feels good to have it done.

So this was a darker story than what I normally write and it was kind of liberating. I used motivations and themes that I wouldn't have had the opportunity to work through otherwise. The main theme running through this book is: is the cost worth the price we pay? We all have to make decisions every day, and especially on the battlefield, but what price do we pay for these choices? And it had a slightly paranormal, apocalyptic thread in it, combining my love of religion with my favorite discussion, the Origin of Evil argument.

Anyway, it's done and I just wanted to share that with you. Back to my other projects and hand receipts. My goodness, the hand receipts will never end!

It's day two without chocolate...

Scrivener My Friend
March 2, 2009

SCRIVENER WAS THE WRITING software that I lusted for before I even knew how to spell revisions. Okay, not really, but I wrote my first three books in Word, which was adequate but somewhat challenging when it came to rearranging huge chunks of text and major revisions (my first book had about six revisions before it reached the version it's in now).

Five books later, and Scrivener is still a writer's best friend. I don't claim to know all of the features, and getting used to writing in sections was a paradigm shift for me, but for the better. And the coolest feature, I just discovered today. I can now color code my notes on the sidebar based on who's POV it's in, which is a super cool feature I've been dying for.

Scrivener also has the note card feature, which allows you to outline on note cards and view them like a storyboard. Then the note cards transform into text segments for when you start writing. If you're an outliner (which I am not) this is a great feature. The other cool feature is the Edit Scrivenings, which combines all the segments into one, so you get the continuity I used to have in Word. It tracks your word count per session, which is awesome for the daily writing challenge from the Austin RWA.

If you're serious about writing, Scrivener is the way to go. I tried several other programs and was not impressed. Scrivener is a perfect fit.

Alas, it only works on a Mac, so unfortunately PC users will have to shift gears to another program. But Literature and Latte offers recommendations for PC users, so all is not lost.

So that's my writing nugget for today. I'm almost done with a book I'd started during last March's writing challenge and had set aside for revisions on that darn first book...which is still clinging to life, despite my efforts to put it under the bed...

The Flag is More than Colored Cloth
March 6, 2009

I'VE ALWAYS BEEN TOUCHED by "Taps," the single bugler alone in the distance at military funerals. Standing at the airfield a few nights ago, I had a profound realization. The US flag.

Now as a soldier you would think the flag would have always been something I've been proud of and I have been. But now it's personal. Not because I was great friends with the soldiers we've lost so far. But because we've lost soldiers. People I've known and at the very least respected for serving their country during a time of war when most people won't.

So when the coffin, bearing the US flag was carried onto that C-17, it dawned on me. People who burn the flag are entitled to their free speech rights. But what about free speech tells people to be so virulently offensive? Has anyone who's ever lit a match beneath the Red White and Blue thought about the men and women who have died to give them that right? Do they care?

Having stood and saluted that flag, knowing another soldier was on their final flight, touched me in a way that I can't fully explain. As a soldier, I might have to defend someone's right to burn a flag. That doesn't mean I won't lose my damn mind if I ever see it in person.

How Not to Pursue Publication
March 11, 2009

SO IT'S BEEN A year and some change since I decided that I was going to try and sell my books. I immediately wrote "The End" and fired that first query letter (garbage) off to agents everywhere, convinced they would grab my book and I would be on my way.

Ah, delusions of grandeur. Anyone who hasn't started on this journey, let me tell you, you better have thick skin. Rejection is painful and frequent and sometimes, it really hurts. We won't discuss how many queries I've sent out, as that would clue the world into how many rejections I've gotten. Someday when I'm published, I'll write an article about getting published the hard way. The way I've done it.

First, I never listen. I have two fabulous critique partners who both said, mmm, not yet. Don't query yet, it's not quite there. Of course I queried. Of course I was rejected. I'm not one of those writers who searches every query looking for why oh why didn't they love it. I can honestly look back at my first round or six of queries and say, yeah, I needed to get rejected.

And that's okay because the rejections eventually stopped being form letters and started coming with comments. Something like, you're really on to something, or your work is timely and compelling. So with a few well-received comments, I went back to the drawing board (or the blank Scrivening, as it were) and kept going.

I recently sent my newest query letter to an amazing agent who shall remain nameless and she was over the moon about it. Her excitement on my pitch for The Last Sunrise has me pretty excited and as it waits in the queue for its round of editing/revisions, I'm feeling encouraged. I told my husband at chow that this year, I was going to do it. I was going to get an offer this year and I was going to call my dream agent and say, I have an offer, can we work together?

Hey, a girl's got to dream right? No matter what people tell you, writing is hard work. The first words you put on a page will not be the words you end up selling, I can almost promise you that. It's a very rare person who sells their first book. Writing involves editing, revising, rereading, editing some more and finally, when you get it just how you like it, you have to kill your darlings to meet a page limit.

But I honestly don't know what I did with myself before I started writing. I love it. I love that thrill of a new idea that sparks a novel and the race to the finish as I type The End. I finally found something else that fits me as well as the Army: the written word.

Now let's see if I can find an editor to agree.

A New Sport: Fly Tennis
March 12, 2009

ANYONE WHO HAS SPENT a summer in Maine understands about insane black flies. They're everywhere and there is no stopping them. Imagine that times ten, and you've got an idea what the flies are like in Mosul. Not only are they little suicide bombers determined to drive you mad with their incessant buzzing, they are also big enough to carry away a Chihuahua.

Enter the great American pastime: fly tennis. The ingenious folks who live in this part of the world have electrified tennis rackets that light up like a doggone fireworks show when you zap a gnat. I can't imagine what zapping a horse fly (or are they camel flies over here?) is going to be like. It might crash the already fragile power grid.

So that's what's new and exciting from Mosul.

The Beauty of Good Shampoo
March 14, 2009

WE'RE IN THE MIDST of one of the worst sandstorms yet. Almost complete brown out.

Anyway, that's not the point. This is: if you've ever traveled somewhere other than the States, you understand the importance of good shampoo. Not just good but the right kind for your hair.

I've been using the wrong shampoo for a little over a month and let's just say that won't happen again. Used the right stuff today and I feel like a new woman. Really.

And please forgive me for not remembering, but whoever sent that Volcano Holiday Blend coffee, that is the best coffee I've had since I've been here. Thank you!

Endless Edits
March 14, 2009

THOSE OF YOU WHO'VE been following the running commentary on my books may know I have a dirty little secret. I can't let go. If I've taken the time to write it, I'm going to edit and revise until it's right.

The first book I ever wrote has undergone at least five rewrites from the first version and is currently set aside, waiting patiently for me to return to it. Which I will. However, book two has currently finished round three of revisions, which is a major improvement when you consider that it happened inside of three months, rather than the year it took for the first one. Since writing that second book, I've finished a total of six novels and am working on number seven.

What have I learned through all this? The first words will very rarely be the last and there is nothing wrong with that. I read somewhere (and I don't know that this is true) that Nora Roberts goes through 3-4 versions of a novel before submitting it and she's one of the best.

I've had to learn one key lesson: kill your darlings. I wrote a scene over a year ago that I loved. Nailed the emotion, the depth, the pain. Loved the ending. My CP read it and said, "the end of this can go."

And you know what? She was right. It was stronger with her suggestions. Much stronger. Just because you love something, don't be afraid to change it or, if it won't submit, cut it. Ruthlessly.

So what does this mean if I'm willing to edit something continually and that means cutting and replacing whole sections, but I won't just cut an entire book? The characters. I can't just force my characters into a box and never see them again. They had a story to be told and I'll keep working at it until I get it right.

Keep at it. Don't give up. Set your work aside and gain some distance from it. And keep editing!

Poo, Meet Fan
March 16, 2009

SO HERE'S A BASIC philosophy of mine regarding briefing the boss bad news. Bad news does not get better with age. If your boss finds out something from a source other than you, you end up looking like an ass. More than likely, if you're trying to hide a problem, the boss is really going to have kittens when he does finally figure it out.

The best course of action when dealing with bad news is to figure out what's going on, come up with a plan, and brief the boss on courses of action that will get the problem solved. Waiting until it's a crisis isn't proper management.

I'd love to hear other thoughts on how to manage and break bad news and different points of view. Always up to learning something new.

Later!

In the Absence of Orders...
March 17, 2009

SO THERE'S THIS THING called the NCO Creed. Every NCO learns it from the earliest days of their careers and most NCO's try to outline what it calls for. There is one line that states: I will take initiative in the absence of orders.

Apparently, that doesn't apply to officers. And, fully understanding that I'm being cryptic here, that's all I'm really going to say on the matter.

29

However, I have some awesome news to report. My new platoon kicks ass! You know, when I was enlisted, I used to think that when officers said they were excited to be somewhere, that they were full of it. Well, I can now say I really am excited to be part of my platoon.

Here's the short version. Professional development has been sorely lacking and so one of the things I instituted was a reading, writing, public speaking program. Needless to say, some of the guys were not happy about getting outside their comfort zone, so we called a platoon meeting to let them air their grievances. These guys impressed the hell out of me. They stated what they didn't like. For instance, the Chief of Staff of the Army's reading list was a little too advanced for most of their levels, but could we use a different reading list? Absolutely.

My guys offered up creative suggestions to still meet the intent and the best part is they bought in on the entire project, once they explained what they wanted to do. Now there are a few who still don't want to do it, and that's fine. But, the majority of the platoon is on board and willing to give it a go.

How awesome is that! My platoon rocks!

Update: What's Really Important
April 4, 2009

BEING IN IRAQ IS kind of like being in prison. Why on earth would I make a comparison like that? Does that mean the Army is like prison? Absolutely not! I love the Army and am proud to be a part of something like the history we're building here. However, comma, there are some striking similarities between being deployed to Iraq and being in prison.

No family. Which means no distractions. No laundry, no dishes to wash, no dog to walk. You go to work, you go home. There's nothing to do but work out, go to work, and sleep. As in prison, Iraq is a good time to get some college work done as there is no reason why a good distance-learning class can't take up at least part of your day.

Iraq is also like prison because you can't leave. Oh you might want to. You'll make plans for all the things you'll do when you get home, but ultimately, you're here for a set period of time and you're not going anywhere. And if you screw up and get fired and sent to another unit, you're going to be here even longer.

So a word to the civilians out there: Iraq is a time for soul searching, for getting to know God, but more importantly for getting to know yourself. You learn what's really important. Family. Time. Those are the things that Iraq takes away from you. But we are part of something larger than ourselves and what we are doing over here is critically important for the success and safety of our nation, unlike, say, prison.

So thank a soldier tonight when you can hug your kids and know they won't get blown up by an IED on their way to school. Try not to get frustrated when you're standing in line at the grocery store, getting food for your family.

Try to remember what's really important.

Mommy, I Want You to Come Home
April 7, 2009

REALLY, WHAT CAN YOU say to that? What four year old is going to understand the Army assignments process and the myriad of reasons her Mommy can't come home right now.

It's been a rough couple of days over here. I've been in typical denial for me, which means avoiding calling home because it just hurts too damn much. Plus the internet over here sucks and the video calls I've been attempting have been fleeting half pictures and choppy audio. So I get an email from mom that says my oldest has been acting out.

So I picked up the phone.

As hell goes, this was a good dry run. My oldest sat a few feet away from the phone wailing, "I want my momma." Then my little one starts crying because the oldest takes the phone away.

Let me tell you, there's nothing quite like hearing your kids hurting and knowing there's nothing you can do about it.

But we got through it. My oldest was distracted by promises of Texas Roadhouse and a promise to call tomorrow.

And I guess that's going to have to be good enough because there are still a lot of tomorrows to get through before we go home.

Black Out
April 12, 2009

AS MANY OF YOU saw, we lost some of our boys this past Good Friday. To say it makes for a somber Easter is an understatement. Anyway, I'm not going to comment on everything that the military does when we lose someone over here but I figured I can explain a little bit.

The first thing we do is take down all outside communications everywhere on the base that we control. That means no internet, no email, no phone calls back to the States or Germany or Korea or anywhere else. Why? Because early in the war, soldiers would call their buddies' wives or families and tell them about their loss before the military could do the notification properly. And that's wrong.

It's wrong because we do things for a reason. Imagine getting a phone call from your spouse's friend and being told that your loved one is gone. You're alone in your home. Or maybe you're at the grocery store. Either way it goes, you get a phone call, and then it's over, but you still have grief to work through, decisions to make, and long days ahead.

Now if we do it the right way, we send a chaplain and a casualty notification officer. While the sight of two uniformed soldiers walking up to your doorstep is a giveaway to what's coming, they are trained to deal with grief, to accept however you react and help you through the initial process. The casualty assistance officer stays with the family for as long as they request him or her to stay, helping through the military system, the funeral arrangements, and the grief process as well.

We don't abandon our family members after we lose a loved one. Mistakes are made, we are after all a human system, with all of those human frailties. But we do everything in our power to make sure we honor our soldiers who made the ultimate sacrifice. And part of that includes keeping people from being told the wrong way.

Blackout is a pain for those of us who don't know the soldiers who died, but it's the right thing to do. People do funny things when they're grieving and it's better not to take the risk. I won't violate blackout to post a blog entry or anything like that.

I fire off a quick email to my kids right before we blackout so my mom doesn't freak out from not hearing from us, but then I wait, just like everyone else, for the notification to be made. It's not convenient, but then again, the right thing to do often isn't.

Combat Loss
April 14, 2009

I'VE DEBATED ABOUT SHARING this email but I figured if folks really want some insight into the emotions and challenges over here in Iraq, I'd be dishonest not to post it.

A few days ago, our unit lost five soldiers in a suicide truck bombing. It was a catastrophic blow for our unit but eventually we all pick up and continue the mission. I didn't know any of the men who died on Good Friday, but I knew PFC Sarandrea and I knew LTC Derby both of whom we lost a few weeks ago. I was not close with either of them but for some reason, their loss and the loss of our other soldiers since we've been here has bothered me tremendously.

I felt inappropriate feeling their loss. I felt like because I wasn't close with these soldiers that I had no right to mourn their passing. So I reached out and asked someone for some advice. I emailed Lieutenant Commander Heidi Kraft, author of Rule Number 2: Lessons I Learned in Combat Hospital, who has been kind enough to correspond with me while I've been over here. Her book was more than inspirational to me; her work helped me laugh when I was first over here and missing my girls more than I can describe.

Anyway, I emailed her a few days ago and asked her about what I was feeling. After requesting her permission, I decided to post my email and her answers here.

It's about as honest as I can get.

Hi Heidi,

I was wondering if you could answer a question for me. Up here in Mosul, we've had several deaths this year. I've known a couple of the folks, in that I worked with them and interacted with them but I wasn't terribly close to any of them. So why do I feel an inappropriate amount of loss? I feel like by grieving for our soldiers we've lost that I'm, I don't really know, fake? But it really bothers me more than I feel like I have a right to be bothered. Any chance you can help me understand that? My husband lost a girl he worked with on a daily basis and he took it hard but I took it worse than he did (at least it looked that way). I don't understand why I have this grief for people I'm not close to and I don't know what to do with it.

Thanks in advance for any help you can offer.

All the best,

Jess

Hi Jess,

I understand completely. Think of my book, when I describe sobbing uncontrollably when I learned Dunham had died. I didn't know him at all. There is something so intense about sharing the bond of combat with someone...it brings people closer in a way that someone who has not deployed would never understand. You are feeling the loss of all Americans in any war, as well as the loss of specific comrades, who, while not necessarily close friends, represented everyone you serve with up there...and yourself. They remind us of the very real danger of combat, and the fragility of human life in combat... and they make us feel vulnerable. The feeling is not just grief...it's guilt, and fear, and loss and helplessness, rolled into one.

But it's normal. Hang in there, Jess.
Godspeed.
Heidi

If Romance Is So Bad, Why Are Sales Strong?
April 18, 2009

RECENTLY, IN INDUSTRY ARTICLES, both the New York Times and others have provided commentary on strong romance sales. Romance behemoth Harlequin is one of the few publishers reporting growth for the last two quarters when other areas of publishing are struggling.

On the flip side, there have been articles basically making fun of the romance genre as "bodice rippers," a misnomer that extends from romance novels of the seventies and eighties where, ahem, Fabio, was made famous. Thankfully, we've moved to significantly more diverse covers but that's just one thing that has changed about the romance genre over the years.

The thing that bothers me is that other authors, either privately or in very public forums, denounce romance as 'not real writing' or just trashy smut. So it's not the next Steinbeck. So what? Milton and Brontë aren't for everyone. Sometimes, simple and sweet is just what someone wants. They don't want the heavy drama of literary fiction. There's nothing wrong with that.

The thing that folks who write these articles forget is that just because you don't like something doesn't mean that someone else doesn't. Their likes and dislikes are just as valid to them as yours are to you. It takes just as much work to write a Harlequin/Silhouette Special Edition as it does to write the next NYT bestseller. Oh, and there are multiple NYT bestsellers who started with Harlequin. It may be looked down on by people as formulaic but the bottom line is that formula sells, even in tough economic times.

Romance is the one genre where there truly is someone for everyone. So you want books about military men? Done. Vampires? Also done. Just about anything you're looking for can be found in the romance genre.

Before you knock down a romance writer as a not real writer, ask him or her why they put those words on paper. Why was that the story they needed to write? The answers might surprise you. But even if you never ask the question, please don't knock romance writers as 'not real' or somehow substandard. It's insulting and it's ignorant of the facts: at the end of the day, romance has been around for a long time, and, looking at current economic trends, it's here to stay.

Check out the diverse world of romance writers. You might be surprised by what you find.

Cyber-Karma
April 20, 2009

I'M A FIRM BELIEVER in what you send out into the world will come back on you. Call it karma or whatever you want, but the bottom line is that I believe if you are a negative person, you will attract negativity. That's one of the reasons that I absolutely adore the folks in the Austin Romance Writers of America. Everyone there is helpful and supportive and always willing to lend a hand or a shoulder. We have a ton of laughs and we welcome published and unpublished alike. The group is fantastic. When I first started going to the meetings, I was apprehensive because I'd never been around a large group of women, let alone civilian women. But I was soon hooked on the laughs and the mommy stories and all-in-all the fun of the group. They made me feel welcome and since I've been over here in Iraq, I get care packages from them on a regular basis. They made me feel like I belong, which is something new for me and I have their support even though I'm thousands of miles away.

The overall positive support I and others get from groups such as the Austin RWA is surprising and it shouldn't be. But it is. I was just on Amazon the other day leaving feedback for a book I've recently read. It's phenomenal and I highly recommended it. But here's the thing. There was a 1-star review. Now, the reviewer is completely within his or her rights to not like the book and to leave not so glowing feedback. But the feedback was complaining about the price of the Kindle version of the book. There was even a comment, I assume, directed at the author, saying that if the price was lowered on the Kindle version, they would remove their negative rating.

Excuse me? We've resorted to blackmailing authors who have no control over the price retailers sell their books for? It's perfectly okay to not like a book and tell everyone why you dislike it. I disagree with that technique, but hey, it's your karma. But why on earth would you post something like that when the author has no control over it?

I guess it's a natural extension of the negativity we've got in the public forum. We tear down teenage starlets because it's fun to watch them fall. And we tear down authors because, well, just because we can.

I propose this to everyone out there who has Facebook, MySpace, or any other blog. Post something positive about someone you don't know. A movie, a book, a band, that bully in high school who's amazingly successful. Send some positive karma into cyberspace and see what happens. Maybe we can turn some of this negativity into something positive. And remember, nothing in cyberspace is anonymous.

I've been tempted many times to rant and rave here about things at work that have pissed me off. For the most part, I've restrained myself. Names have not been named even if scenarios have been discussed (or vented about). I'm working on that on my end.

The next time you think about dropping a negativity bomb onto the internet, remember, it's easy to find out who you are. Why don't you try to be a little more polite?

Book Update
April 23, 2009

SO I ALREADY TWEETED about it but my eighth book is nearing a close. Night shift has turned out to be incredibly productive for my muse (too bad it won't last when I go back on days/go back to the States). I count Burning Out as my eighth, even though I've only got seven books listed because it's a completely new book. New conflict, new plot. The only thing that isn't new is about 2000 words and the characters. Otherwise, it's new.

So if I've written all these books, why aren't I selling them? When I went back and looked at the first draft of Burning Out (because I hadn't touched it in nearly a year since I finished it) there were no less than fourteen plot points (and I stopped counting about a third of the way through). So I trashed it. I looked at all the different issues I had running through that book and picked two and started weaving them together and started over.

The second reason is that even though I've gone through my books each day after I finished a section, they're still a first draft. I need a second set of eyes and both of my critique partners are neck deep in deadline insanity. So for the first time since

I decided I was a writer, I'm practicing patience (NOT my strong suit).

The stories keep coming and the writing every day certainly helps. I keep waiting for the stories to dry out but they don't. Some have more fire than others, in that I can't put it down and I know where it's going, others are a slow burn that keep going despite myself. Burning Out was a little of both. The characters called to me but I didn't know their story. Once I started, it was a slow crunch each day to see what was going to happen next. I hit my midpoint snag that I always do around 30K words but pushed through it and am happy to say we're nearing 80K a few days later.

Writing keeps me sane over here. So I'll continue to write on new stuff until I either (a). go home, or (b). have something sold. More on that, hopefully soon.

The Worst Idea *Ever*
April 26, 2009

APPARENTLY, I HAVE A masochistic streak. A mean one. Yesterday, at the urging of my good friend Al and my chaplain, I finally finished The Shack. Which prompted a panic attack at the thought of my children getting lost at the circus and me asking my parents not to take them. There isn't quite enough drama in our lives so I had to throw that in. Hopefully, my four year old will be able to understand that mommy is just paranoid somewhere in all the therapy she's going to require from growing up with us as parents (there's more, just wait).

The second worst thing I did was my hubby and I decided to watch Marley and Me. Now, for those of you who know us, you know we have very special dogs. Special being the operative word. Watching Marley was like watching our Robbie, running away down the beach, destroying the house and yes, watching the poop (popsicle sticks in our case, not necklaces).

So why is this a bad thing? I started crying at the opening credits and really let it go by the end. I cried while laughing my ass off over that dog. Robbie is no longer with us, which made the end of that movie especially rough.

Now, I'm sitting in my CHU with two Dr Pepper cans up to my eyes, trying to get the swelling to go down. My husband is bringing me back dinner so I didn't have to go out in public. I look like I've been beat up (crying jags will do this). Watching Marley and Me, while missing your kids and your pets in Iraq: Worst Idea Ever.

The Panic Has Passed - For Now
April 30, 2009

THERE'S NOTHING QUITE LIKE being 3000 miles from home and having a panic attack about your four year old trying to feed your two year old because something has happened to their primary caregiver, AKA my mom. My mother is one of the healthiest folks I know, but after the announcement of the swine flu, yep, good old-fashioned panic attack.

Called on a good friend of mine, Robin Shepherd, to help and she worked me through the worst of it. Let me tell you, I would probably be sitting in my CHU, plotting my escape from Iraq had Robin not calmed me down.

The single hardest part about being over here is surrendering my ability to care for my children as a mother. Rationally, I know that me being with my kids has absolutely no impact on whether or not they get sick. But the thought of anything happening to them is just unbearable.

It's kind of like when our dog Robbie died. He was being well cared for when some sick and twisted soul decided to feed him antifreeze. Robbie was a good dog. Dumb as a box of rocks, which explains why he was chowing down on antifreeze while our other dog Megan was telling him to leave it alone (another story for another time). I'm not busted up over the fact that he had to be put down. By the time a vet was willing to treat him, it was too late. What kills me is that my dog died alone, in a strange hospital, and he had no idea that we still loved him.

That's what I worry about while I'm over here. That something will happen and I won't be there to provide mom-comfort. I'm coping now and have a great idea for a book that rose out of this panic attack, but for my mental health's sake, I'm going to not write it while I'm over here. My brigade surgeon is already taking notes on the odd questions I ask.

I'm better now. But now I have a good idea what soul-crushing panic feels like.

Speed Racer
May 1, 2009

I WRITE TOO FAST. Hell, half the time, I talk too fast, too. But in writing, my fingers go fast but my brain goes faster. I have no idea how I went from never having finished a story to having seven novels under my belt, but I did.

So why is that a problem?

It's not, in a classic sense. My issue is that getting that first draft out comes in a rush but so do the revisions. And revisions, in my case, need to take a lot longer than they do. I'm currently revising Shattered for an amazing agent who I'm flattered has even given me the time of day and I'm slowing down.

How? For starters, I'm reading out loud. That in and of itself has done wonders for picking up dropped words, non sequitur phrases, and wordy sentences. Secondly, I'm trying to read the story like I've never seen it before.

Reading out loud, though, is the best idea I've ever had suggested to me. And the other thing: revisions are a good thing. I used to fear revisions. Now, I'm good with them. I enjoy them. In fact, I think I like editing more than I like getting new words on the page. I love seeing a story go from raw idea to something actually (I hope) readable.

So I'm slowing down. And, fingers crossed, it will make a difference.

Top 10 Things I'm Glad I Brought to Iraq
May 5, 2009

SO YOU MIGHT BE wondering, what does a girl need to survive over here? I'm going to automatically exclude my husband from the list of top ten things I'm glad I brought to Iraq because that goes without saying. But, all things being equal, here's my list so far:

10. Lansinoh. "Oh really?" you might ask. Why exactly do you need a cream designed for nursing moms in Iraq? Two words: Chapped Lips. The weather over here is absolutely brutal and nothing heals chapped lips faster than Lansinoh. Once you get past the slightly off taste (hey if you nursed, your baby ate it, it's fine), it is the single best cream on the planet for getting lips beyond the dry chapped look that is so in vogue over here.

9. Clinique SPF 15 Glosswear. Because Lansinoh does not have SPF. Enough said. Clear is functional and lets me feel a little bit like a girl. At least that's what I keep telling myself. Hey, my husband is here with me.

8. Flip Flops. Here's a visual for you: public showers. Nasty public showers. The kind that are so dirty the little Lamisil Monster won't even attend. Flip flops are the last bastion of protection between your feet and a case of fungus you won't be able to kill with bleach.

7. InCase Covers. I'm a gadget geek. I lusted after a Kindle until I bought my iPod Touch (see #6). I have an InCase cover for my MacBook (see #1), all my portable hard drives, and my iPod. They've kept the dust down to way below normal levels. If you're coming over here and care about your electronics, get these little neoprene cases. They're worth their weight in gold. (Trust me, the dirt is unreal.)

6. iPod Touch. Why not a regular iPod? Why not an iPhone? iPod Touch has Skype, so I can call home (once my headphones with mic show up) on wifi. I have pics of my kids with me wherever I go (I look at them more than you think). Plus, books via Stanza (free), news via NYT (free) and USA Today (also free and my hubby thought those two apps were the coolest ever), movies, and of course, music for those hours at the gym on the Stairmaster and elliptical trainer reading all of ARWA's fabulous author's books.

5. Clinique Daily Defense SPF 25. I stood on the airfield for 2 hours with no headgear on and did not get a sunburn. Proof enough that my favorite multitasking moisturizer is worth its weight in gold.

4. Headlamp from OCS. We had to do night land navigation in OCS. At Fort Benning. In July. There are some big-ass spiders in the Fort Benning woods.

(I was not a happy girl. Just ask my mom about the 4:30 am phone call where the spider was blocking my path and demanding ransom.) In comes the headlamp. One hand for the map, one hand for the spider stick (don't ask), and you've got a much happier (and sane) officer candidate. And while my headlamp sat in my duffle bag for a year, it has since resurrected its usefulness during this deployment.

3. Birth Control. Because nothing is worse than going on a deployment with a whole year's worth of birth control, even if your husband is going to be with you in the same CHU. And nothing says neurotic like wondering if you're pregnant every month because you screwed up your pills. Ah, the joys of being a woman in a combat brigade. Maybe I should go to the ladies' tea.

2. Tide. Because nothing says eww more than getting back dirty clothes from the laundry point. Drop a capful of Tide into the bag and presto, clothes that almost smell like home. Now if only I could do something about the dingy yellow of my socks.

1. MacBook. Two words: Time Machine. Knock on wood, no data has been lost in the making of this journey and the Apple gods willing, none will. Create my website, blog, call home with video conferencing on Skype, and write my next book on Scrivener. This little sucker has the power and beauty to meet all my computer geek needs. But that's not the best part. Again with the dust? The aluminum unibody has kept the dust remarkably

out of the important parts. I opened it up yesterday to see how it was holding up and I was pleasantly shocked to see that there was barely any dust in there at all. Yay, Apple.

These are the things you will find either on me or near me at all times during this fun little adventure in Iraq. I'd love to hear other things folks consider in their top ten of things to bring to Iraq.

Is It Bad To Be A Mac?
May 7, 2009

MY OTHER HALF AND I were involved in a discussion the other day, which got me thinking. I was simply commenting about how I really love my MacBook. He made the comment that using Macs was typical of what was wrong with America. Which was to say it was blatant consumerism at its best when you're paying for a brand rather than the best product out there (let's not forget he bought it for me as a deployment gift but I digress).

What I explained to him is not that my computer is superior because it's the base line MacBook but that it gives me functionality I don't have on a PC: namely Scrivener and iLife. He pointed out that I could get more power for significantly less money, which is true, except that I wouldn't have Scrivener. I wouldn't have Time Machine and a whole slew of other Mac programs. But mostly Scrivener. Lusting after Scrivener is what ultimately made the switch easy for me.

For me, my MacBook has made my life simpler. I no longer worry that I'm going to lose all my data and I've been using it for six months straight and I've yet to have a single issue. (There have been a few hiccups but nothing that Time Machine or Google didn't help me identify in a few minutes.) There has been no lost data (meaning completed novels that disappear into the ether, knock on wood).

So I ask you: am I being a snob simply because I enjoy using my computer? I like the feel of the keys, the quickness of the startup (open the lid) and shut down (close the lid). Does that make me a brand-conscious snit or someone who simply doesn't feel like digging into the control panel to change power settings when I can press a button?

My MacBook is not superior (though Consumer Reports says it is). It is simply enjoyable, functional, and reliable. What more could a deployed writer ask for?

The "Context" of Combat
May 8, 2009

HERE'S ANOTHER ONE OF those posts I try not to make too often. It was announced today that Stephen Green, the man accused of raping and murdering 14 year old Abeer Qassim al-Janabi in Iraq, was convicted of rape and murder, and now faces sentencing.

I am glad this animal was found guilty.

Green's attorney urged the jury to "consider the 'context' of war," saying soldiers in Green's unit of the 101st Airborne Division lacked leadership.

Here's my problem with that. This lawyer is asking civilians to understand the context of war. Which is fine, except that this case does not need to be viewed in the context of a wartime environment.

In what case is it morally acceptable for our soldiers to rape and murder children and their families? There is absolutely no justification for Green's actions and the actions of the cowards who went with him that night.

Do not mistake the actions of soldiers in the haze of battle who misidentify a target, with the actions of a criminal who planned a brutal rape and murder.

War asks that good men do bad things. Green and his lackeys were not good men doing bad things. They represent the worst of our society and unfortunately, they were not stopped in time to prevent this tragedy. I am truly sorry for the actions of these soldiers.

I am even more sorry that their attorney has the audacity to explain this brutal crime as the impact of combat stress. It's a shame that the media plays into this and casts doubts on the honor of our men and women in uniform by lumping us in with this criminal.

When the media repeat the lawyer's argument that this should be "considered in the context of war" they do every honorable man and woman in the military a great disservice.

Disappointing Title
May 9, 2009

THERE'S NOTHING QUITE SO frustrating as finally settling on a title for your book, that you've worked on forever, only to find that a NYT best-selling author has a book with the same title and the same hero: a wounded GI. Ah well, back to the title drawing board. At least my hero isn't a pilot, too. That's another book.

Happy Mother's Day
May 10, 2009

HAPPY MOTHER'S DAY, EVERYONE. Today is one of those days I want to sleep through, because if I don't I'm liable to spend an inordinate amount of it crying.

But I have to say there are some great moms out there, but I've got one of the best. Not only did she take my two heathen kids for us for a year, but she's doing a damn fine job raising them (trust me, my oldest could piss off the Pope). I'm able to be here in Iraq and do my job because my mom is taking care of business back home.

Thanks, Mom, for being a great mom and an even better Grammy!

I love you.

Pictures or Not?
May 14, 2009

THE MORE I PAY attention to the news, the more I feel the urge to comment on things that are probably going to get me into trouble. But here goes anyway.

I think the President made a smart move not releasing the additional pictures of Abu Ghraib. For those who disagree, sign up for the Army or Marines and come walk the street with our boys. The people in those pictures have been punished and held to account, of that I am fairly certain. The only thing those pictures serve to do is inflame the media and the bias that is already against us in the Arab world.

In case you've forgotten—and I assure you the Muslim world has not—Abu Ghraib is still a rallying cry around the region. Releasing more photos would only serve to give greater incentive to those who wish to die blowing us up along with them.

Whatever those pictures show, I'm sure they highlight the flaws of a few, not the consent of the many. We are an organization made up of people, humans who make mistakes, and contrary to what people may believe, we are not an organization of bloodthirsty baby killers. We have true believers among us, who believe in the morality and righteousness of what they are doing. We do not condone these actions and when they are discovered, we deal with the perpetrators. We learned many lessons from Abu Ghraib. Let's not make soldiers who have nothing to do with the situation pay for the choices of a few.

Once more, I challenge those of you who would question the soldiers on the ground: Join Us. Send your son or daughter over here to live with the fear of mortars and rockets and VBIEDs. Of losing friends who walk the streets. Experience making those events for yourself, then sit back and say release the photos. And once more, I tell you we are not perfect. We make mistakes. We more than most have to live with the consequences of our decisions, because they are life-altering and more often than not, they are permanent.

Thus far, the President has had to make some difficult choices and I applaud his efforts. He made a balanced decision about the photos of our Fallen Heroes, probably the best choice that could be made under the circumstances.

I think he made the right one here and our boys on the streets will not face an increased threat because of it. For now, anyway.

Disclaimer - In Case You Missed It
May 19, 2009

THIS BEARS REPEATING. I'VE said it before but just so we're clear. Anything said on this blog by me represents my opinion, unless otherwise specifically cited as belonging to someone else. Nothing I say should be misconstrued to speak for the US Government, US Army, or Department of Defense.

Also, please bear in mind, everything I post has been scrubbed for OPSEC. I'm not going to post anything about operations or anything else spicy or scandalous. Nor will you find that in my tweets or on Facebook. I'm highly conscious of what I put out here and will post nothing that detracts from our mission over here.

That being said, the few times I do voice my opinion about certain issues, they are mine. I'm not a spokesperson for anyone other than myself and I am no one's mouthpiece. Those of you who know me already know I'm pretty opinionated, but I do censor myself here so as not to bring discredit upon my unit, my profession, or my nation.

I won't post anything here that I wouldn't want my mother, my soldiers, or my superiors reading.

I'll talk about things from a romance writer's perspective, which, let's face it, involves gender issues, sex, and other areas of intimacy. But please know, I'm very conscientious about what I post.

That's all. Just in case you missed it.

Why Am I Having Such a Hard Time With My Young Adult?
May 19, 2009

SO, THOSE OF YOU who have been following me know that I'm working on a young adult paranormal. It's my first foray into YA and other than the Twilight Series and Harry Potter, I haven't read any.

Yeah, it's a great idea to try and write something you have no idea about. But I digress.

This book is kicking my ass and I think I figured out why. In my adult novels, I'm not pulling my punches. If a throat needs to be cut—figuratively of course—then so be it. If my characters move to a point where they have sex, yup, all fine and good.

But in this one, I'm trying to get into the head of a seventeen-year-old girl who has been made an outcast in her school. Her friends are having sex. Her little sister is playing the choking game, albeit unwillingly. And I read several scathing articles about some of the popular YA books out there that venerate sex, money, and popularity like nothing else. It's Mean Girls times a hundred.

Again, I say that having not read any of these books—though I plan on it so that I have an idea about the market.

Here's my issue: I'm writing a book for kids. Basically, the market for YA is 14 and up. Middle grade is 12-ish. I have two daughters who will someday be reading in the YA market.

I'm hung up on my morality. I'm writing a book that other people's kids are going to read (at least that's the hope), and more than anything, I feel like I have a social responsibility to write something that I would be okay with my own kids reading, right?

I mean, even in my adult novels, when a throat needs to be cut, there's an underlying issue there. I hope my books deal with some tough issues—combat zone choices and their impact, right and wrong, good and bad. Does doing a bad deed make someone a bad person? That kind of thing. So I'm hoping there's substance to my books.

With my YA, I'm pulling back, trying to remember how I felt when I was in high school. What did I think about the girls who were having sex back then—because contrary to popular belief, we all weren't. What do I remember about the "popular" girls?

I want to write a book that talks to those girls who aren't in the clique but who still have value as people even if they aren't the richest, the prettiest or the best at sports. I want to write about a young woman who has to deal with everyone around her doing these things and has to make her own choices because her parents are so wrapped up in their lives, they can't see that their kids still need them.

So what's my problem? In writing this book, I worry that I'm somehow glamorizing what happens to my characters. And yet, I worry that as I write this, people will think I'm condoning what I write about.

I guess we'll see where the story takes me for now. This is one book that has tortured me, though, because I worry about my own daughters reading it. And it would make me the ultimate hypocrite if I put something out there for other people's kids without considering the impact to my own.

Memorial Day: They Have Names
May 25, 2009

REMEMBER THE FALLEN. THEY have names.

I never really got it before. Which is disappointing when you think that I've been a soldier for fourteen years but I never truly understood what Memorial Day was about.

When I was five years old, my brother and I found a hand-sized American flag that had been run over by the lawn mower. I took it to school. My favorite teacher, Ms. Emhoff, took the flag from me and scolded me in front of the entire class. I didn't understand until she told me her brother died in World War II. I should have gotten it then.

I never understood when I would see Vietnam Vets crying at a parade for the fallen. I felt sad for them, but I didn't understand. I didn't understand when I saw an old man at the officer's club wearing his Cav Stetson, just wanting to be around soldiers a little longer. I didn't understand why my Command Sergeant Major lost his mind on a soldier for not shaving. It wasn't about the beard. It was about wearing the uniform with pride, because in these colors, soldiers have died.

I started to understand the day we took our first casualty in country. The day we lost a battalion commander and his crew. I started to understand the first day I stood in the Memorial Ceremony and Taps ripped part of my soul out. And I started to understand the day I stood on the tarmac and saluted a flag-draped coffin. It was the first. Unfortunately, I doubt it will be the last.

I walked into the chow hall today, acting like today was any other day. It was decorated in Red White and Blue.

Alone at the front was a soldier's cross: a Kevlar helmet resting on a rifle, propped up in a pair of empty boots, a pair of dog tags hung around the rifle.

Today I understand that it is not about the flag, or parades, or those of us who are still fighting. Today it is about our fallen brothers and sisters. The ones who gave all for something greater than themselves.

Today I understand. And it hurts.

The Nicest Compliment
May 26, 2009

A FEW WEEKS AGO, I posted how there was another book out there about a wounded GI and it was called Shattered. Well, the author, the fabulous JoAnn Ross, stopped by on my blog and offered some amazing comments. I'm incredibly flattered to have her stop by and read my stuff and it was really great chatting with her. If you've never read them, her High Risk series does an excellent job of capturing military life and she is just one author among many who support the troops over here. She's also one of the few authors brave enough to tackle the issue of our growing family of amputees from the wars over here and she does it with taste and class and treats her hero like he is: a hero. Remember those who also gave so much, too.

I wanted to say thanks to everyone who stopped by yesterday on the blog and commented. It's really heartwarming to prove the media wrong. People still care that there is a war going on. Just look at the comments on Twitter and in the blogosphere. Thank you for caring and for your continued support and we'll see you on the high ground.

Seriously, I'm Neurotic
June 3, 2009

APPARENTLY, I HAVE A genetic predisposition to worry incessantly about something. The constant redesign of my website comes from two things: one, I want it to look like a typical writer's website; and two, I don't want it to look like a typical writer's website. So I continue to worry and stress. I almost had a damn panic attack about this foolish thing before I went to sleep this morning (yes, that means a new site is up).

Several weeks ago, my husband went out in sector with the brigade CSM. I told myself he was going to be fine and I was not going to worry. Yeah, right. I got to my CHU and started imagining getting woken up by The Knock. The worry that I'd open the door and see the chaplain standing there. It got so big in my head, I had to force myself to go to sleep. And when he came in and woke me up to tell me he was back, the relief that crawled across my heart was insane.

You'd think that now I have an agent, things would settle down in my head, right? Wrong. I keep thinking that this is all a dream and that my agent is going to email me one day and say, "oh, so sorry but you misunderstood me."

On the home front, my hubby and I are going on R&R next week and I'm starting to get wound up about that. Not the going home part. Not that first hug at the airport or the constant "Mommy. I want your attention" part. It's the leaving part. I haven't even gone yet and I'm upset about having to come back.

Really? Is this normal? Or am I just going quietly crazy over here, finding things to worry about to keep my mind busy?

Right now, it's 0230 in the morning. I'm going to file my nightly report and then sit down in front of my MacBook and write. I'm hopefully going to channel all this insanity into a character who will be stressed out but sympathetic and hopefully not crazy. You'll have to tell me what you think of her, if she ever gets published.

Beyond Heaving Bosoms
June 5, 2009

EVERY ROMANCE AUTHOR SHOULD read Beyond Heaving Bosoms by the gals at Smart Bitches, but especially new writers, like myself, who stopped reading romance for about a decade, then decided to write one, complete with clichés galore. Why on earth would I recommend a book based on a website called Smart Bitches Who Love Trashy Books? Read on, oh fearless one.

BHB was hysterical but there was also valid social commentary. I mean have you ever read anything about the issue of rape in romance novels in the 70s and 80s? While they cite academic and popular sources, I'd never even given that a thought except that for a while (around the mid 90s), I stopped reading romance novels. I'd read several of the books they mentioned as examples of rape in earlier novels and I remembered those "forced seductions" well, but I'd never really looked at the social context of the topic and it was fascinating.

The Smart Bitches also discuss clichés inside the romance genre in hysterical detail. The book cover mullet nearly had me falling off the Stairmaster, I was laughing so hard. And, while I don't want to spoil the thrill of reading it for yourself, their discussion of the clichés, overcrowded genres, and other tantalizing tidbits make the book beyond worth reading. Had I read it before I started writing my first novel, I might have had a much better idea of things to avoid that were truly character clichés.

Read Beyond Heaving Bosoms. It's funny and I can almost guarantee you'll learn something about the genre we write, read, and love.

Tormented or Well-Adjusted Characters

June 7, 2009

WHICH KIND OF CHARACTER is more compelling to you? The tormented, tortured hero or the well-adjusted, confident male? Is it better to read about a heroine who's got it all and finds something more, or do you enjoy seeing characters who have some emotional baggage to check before they can truly be happy?

I laughed when Smart Bitches, in doing their analysis of romance novel heroes in Beyond Heaving Bosoms, called Vampires "more EMO than you." But that got me thinking. Why are vampires invariably tortured? Did you ever meet a vampire hero who is cool with what he's done? Who has no problems killing and feeding to sustain himself? If you did meet that hero, would he be more or less compelling than the vampire who hates having to take another life just so he can live? Would you want to read about a hero who was completely okay with killing, and would the resolution of his story have him becoming not okay with it?

I recently read a book (not paranormal) that had a female killing two guys who were trying to kill her. I applauded but then was disappointed because she had angst over killing them. In the romance world, it almost seems the norm that our males can have angst over killing but they'll get over it but our females can't kill without major emotional issues and then get permission (more or less) from their significant other for the killing to be okay.

Why is that? Why do we (and I'm including myself in this) write heroes who can be tortured but in the end give themselves permission to be okay with it but we write heroines who need outside permission to do what they did.

I guess what I'm asking is can we love characters who have killed and who are okay with that killing? Can you read about a hero who is not tortured by what he's done? Or a heroine who is okay with killing but who has other issues? Do our characters have to be tortured in order for us to care about them? And if that character is tortured, does it feel like a cheat when they get their HEA by linking up with their soul mate or should there be more to the issue resolution than just the "magic hoo hoo"?

So tell me: do you crave tortured characters or ones who just have issues? Who are your favorite tortured characters? Why? Who are your favorite relatively well-adjusted characters? How do you torture your characters? What issues are most poignant to you as a reader?

Top 10 Things I Won't Miss About Iraq
June 9, 2009

SO I'M LEAVING ON R&R in the next few days and this will probably be the last post I make for a while. Given that I'm going to one of the only houses in the US that does not have internet access, unplugging will probably be painful but good.

In honor of my vacation from the sandbox, I have accomplished a grand total of nothing tonight. Couldn't concentrate on the new book. Couldn't sleep. Really did nothing but drink water in prep for the 120 degree heat in Kuwait.

But, I thought I'd leave you with a few of the things I'm NOT going to miss about Iraq for the next few weeks. Not sure if I'll get to ten or not but here goes.

10. Community showers. There's nothing more disconcerting than walking to the shower and discovering that your favorite shower stall (the one that actually drains right, is not covered in mold, and has decent water pressure) is taken. Then walking back to your CHU and getting covered in dust all over again. Good times.

9. Waiting for my favorite shower stall. Now, I'll only have to share my shower with my children, who I'm sure can't wait to get in the shower with me. Yay, naked baby buns!!

8. Walking to the shower. In flip flops. In the dark. Hoping that the denial about camel spiders and cobras will continue without you (a). stepping on one, or (b). having one jump on you.

7. Being in uniform. I love the Army. I love my uniform and completely respect what it stands for. But damn! I'm ready for girlie clothes and makeup and feeling like a woman again.

6. Not feeling like I'm drawing attention to myself for putting makeup on. Yes, I'm going ultimate girl when I go home and I'm going to glam it up. Course, when I come back to Iraq, it will be back to no makeup and under-eye circles galore.

5. Porta-Potties. Nothing says deployment like the smell of a Porta-Pottie in 110 degree heat. And then finding that there's no toilet paper. Good times.

4. Eye protection. Yes, I'm wearing cute sunglasses when I get home, not the military grade ballistic eyewear that will keep me safe and look like I'm wearing my grandfather's driving glasses.

3. The chow hall. I really don't think this requires clarification.

2. Body armor. It's safe. It's heavy. And it adds 20 degrees to your core body temperature.

1. Briefings. Useless briefings where we read the slides and tell everyone information they already know. Yes. The only reading/briefings I'm doing when I go home is to my kids. I'm going to enjoy the heck out of my time in the States and come back ready to redeploy.

Made It!
June 13, 2009

AFTER TWO DAYS OF travel, finally made it home to Maine. The kids are amazing and so different, it's not even funny. Will post more when I'm not emotionally drained, but wow, it's good to be home. Everything smells so clean and fresh and good here. And I won't even start on how much the girls have changed but will post more some other time. Thanks to everyone who wished us well! More soon!

Going Home Part 1
June 17, 2009

WE STOPPED IN IRELAND on the way home from Iraq. I walked around the airport, simply enjoying being back in civilization. Coffee and bars and duty free shopping. What's funny is that the people around us looked at us like we were a spectacle. One lady asked us where we were coming from and where we were going. She was incredibly nice, her accent gentle and lilting. Another gentleman—we're pretty sure he was American—stopped and shook our hand and said thank you.

But all in all, Ireland was just a comma in my journey back to my kids. I saw a lady walking around the airport with her two little girls. Both blond, both young. The little one was tiny and adorable. It's funny how watching a small child drag a rolling suitcase will inspire tears in random adults but it did. The kids were so adorable and a longing I cannot fully describe began burning in my chest. When people say their hearts ache, do you know what they mean? The anticipation wraps around me and brings tears to my eyes. Just a few more hours and I'll be home. I'm not even there yet but the thought of going back to Iraq is breaking my heart.

So I do what I always do. I shut it down and turn it off and cling to the anticipation of seeing my babies. Of the fights and the hugs and the kisses and the laughter. If our recently adopted horse (aka Lilly, the 100 pound yellow lab refugee who joined our family from a rescue shelter) is going to remember us. Have our cats gone feral living with my brother-in-law?

And what about the kids? Will they understand that Mommy and Daddy have to go again? Will they be angry and lash out, destroying their rooms and the story books I've made for them? Will they kick the dog because they don't know what to do with the hurt inside of them?

All I know is that our choice has been made and our kids have to live with the impact of our choices. I hope and pray that it's the right choice and that in the long run, the girls will be okay and that in a few more months we'll be a family again.

Notions of patriotism seem kind of far off when your daughter is wailing into the phone that she wants to go home. I hope she understands someday. Because hope and prayer are about all I've got to cling to.

Day Three
June 18, 2009

WE'VE BEEN HOME FROM Iraq for a few days now. It's incredible. The worries that I had about the kids being confused or my youngest being more attached to Grammy and not wanting anything to do with me were unfounded. I know it breaks my mom's heart that the girls are utterly and completely reattached to us and it's terrible how cruel an almost three year old can be. But the kids are doing great. They're happy and well-adjusted and aren't out-of-control little monsters (good job, Mom, seriously).

My youngest is a little clingy, which is doubly surprising for me because she's always done her own thing. Now she walks up: "Mommy, I want you to pick me up." And she snuggles right up. Her vocabulary is incredible now. We're talking full sentences and comprehension that's just insane. My oldest is polite and considerate and, shock: they both listen (for the most part). I'm sure it's just a honeymoon phase but I'm absolutely thrilled at how they're doing.

I'm pretty sure my heart is going to shatter when I get ready to go back to Iraq. We've slipped right back into being a family so quickly that having to give all that up again for a few more months is going to beyond suck. But it will go by quickly as we get busy with redeployment and my oldest starts school. Christmas will be here before we know it and the year will have gone by in a blink.

I feel a lot better having seen how the kids are coping. My oldest has some anger issues and she cries at the slightest provocation but together we've figured out that she just needs to be held. It's what both girls seem to want more than anything: Mommy snuggles. And that, in and of itself feels so incredibly good. They still love me: they haven't forgotten me and they haven't stopped loving me. The fact that I have to leave again is brutal but I'm relatively sure it's going to be okay. We shall see how this experiment plays out in the long run but right now, it just feels so damn good to be home!

Happiness
June 20, 2009

HAPPINESS IS DREAMING YOU'RE already back in Iraq from R&R only to wake up and discover you have ten days left in the States with your kids.

Becoming Mommy Again
June 21, 2009

IT'S AMAZING HOW QUICKLY everything falls back into the same old patterns. The honeymoon is over and just like that, both girls once more are just kids instead of the kids of deployed parents and I'm just a mom, instead of a soldier mom with a truckload of mommy guilt. I've discovered a lot hasn't changed since I've been gone and some things I don't think that ever will.

For instance, I've accepted the fact that I will never again be able to go to the bathroom by myself. There is no way my almost three year old is willing to let me out of her sight. She might be attached to Mommy by a very short string but she doesn't want anything to do with Daddy, hence Mommy is on call all day every day. And since my four year old is now too old to go to the bathroom with Daddy, it's all Mommy all the time. Which leads to some long lines in the ladies' room and hopefully, other moms understand what's taking so long (you can't beat a two year old off the potty with a stick if she's determined to go poopie).

My four year old is very much a Daddy's girl except when it comes to bedtime. Then she wants Mommy snuggles. I can't tell you how touched I was that both girls wanted me to "nuggle" with them as they fall asleep at night. And what's funny is that I have nothing more important to do than 'nuggle until they fall asleep. I wouldn't trade eight hours of uninterrupted sleep in Iraq for the fits and turns I get here with one ear always listening for the girls. Of course, I've also found the cure for insomnia: chasing two kids around nonstop from 6 am til 8 pm (or thereabouts).

The biggest thing that has changed is that when my girls want my time, they get it. While it might feel like everything is back to normal with us, I know that it's not. I have a very short amount of time with them right now and the only thing I can do to make the next five months easier on them is give them every bit of time that I can.

And that's a change in me as Mommy that I think will get me a lot down the road with my relationship with my daughters.

The Value of Time
June 22, 2009

IT'S PRETTY SAD THAT it took me going to Iraq to truly appreciate the one thing I can never get back: time. My two year old has changed so much since we've been gone. She talks up a storm now. When we left, she'd just had tubes put in her ears and was discovering her vocal talents. Now? Now she talks from the moment she gets up until she goes to sleep and she's funny! I think 2-3 is my favorite age. We loved our oldest at that age and our youngest is truly a character. Granted, there are challenges, such as a staunch refusal to potty train but that's okay.

We walked down the beach today with the girls. They were picking up seashells and running through the waves (well, one of them was, the other one was terrified of the water and spent much of the walk on Mommy's shoulders) and I was just there, in the moment. Not worried about anything else. We'd get where we were going when we got there. So my oldest got soaked. Oh well. I was just there, in the moment, enjoying watching my girls and that's something that I haven't truly been able to do in the past. I always had my mind going on something, worried about this or that.

Time is the one thing I can never get back. I won't get this time back that I've spent in Iraq. This is a year of my daughters' lives I'll never get to live. It's a part of the sacrifice that we make for our country and for our families. Knowing that we're part of something bigger than ourselves, however, doesn't make it any easier to hear your two year old say, "I miss you very much, Mommy."

I won't ever get this time back, but I damn sure will make the most of every minute from now on.

Things Iraq Has Taught Me
June 23, 2009

IT'S FUNNY BUT BEING in Iraq has been somewhat liberating as a woman. There are no mirrors there. At least, there aren't that many. I spend all day at work and other than in the latrine or in our CHU or the gym, there aren't mirrors to speak of. I once was obsessed with my appearance. Now that I'm home, I still want to look and feel like a woman but I'm different now. I won't lie and tell you that the two days I was home and had to wear my mom's clothes and my husband's sweats I wasn't bothered with feelings of frumpiness. But now that I have my own clothes, things are different.

Before I would constantly check my makeup, my clothes, or critically look at myself in the mirror. I would stress if my hair was a wreck or if I hadn't covered a blemish.

Now, I get dressed, put on makeup, and go. If a mirror shows up, I check but how I look is no longer a major time-consuming thought. I picked up clothes that I like, that fit, and that are comfortable and that's it. I'm dressed, I'm made up and I'm going.

It's kind of weird for me to be able to get dressed and truly go. I'm a former fat girl (and on my way there again if I don't get my ass in the gym but that's another story), but no matter what, I've always worried about how I look since I've been an adult. For me to be low maintenance in my head is a huge change and one that I'm grateful for. I won't say that being in Iraq has been liberating because I think that's the wrong word, but wearing nothing but ACUs and PTs for months on end has definitely changed my perspective on things.

And I think it's for the better.

The Worst Night Ever
June 25, 2009

SO WE'RE BACK AT Grammy's now and the girls are settled right back in. Leave has actually gone very well. The girls have had a blast and I for one, have been focused on letting go of rigid parenting (like normal bedtimes) and just enjoying my time with the girls. For the most part, the kids have done a fantastic job adjusting and slipping back into family mode.

Or so I thought.

Tonight, Mommy tried to get an hour of Mommy time to visit with her long-time high school friend. I figured I'd been nothing but Mommy from the minute I walked through the door and I had gladly enjoyed every single minute. But I also figured that being back at Grammy's, the girls would relax a little and be a little less clingy.

Boy, was that a mistake. Within a few minutes of me not being in the room, both girls were crying and screaming. By the time they'd cried it out, their little eyes were all puffy and red and I'd won the worst parent in the world award.

My oldest wrapped her arms around my neck and said, "Mommy, things aren't going to be the same without you here." Then it dawned on me. While we were in Delaware, the girls were having fun and pretending that we really were a family again. Now that we're back at Grammy's and not heading back to Texas, reality has struck both of them like the 18-wheeler Grammy drives: Mommy and Daddy are leaving again. Time is such an adult concept that my kids don't have any way of really counting down other than to look forward to winter and sometime around Christmas for us to come home.

It really busted me up tonight taking even that small amount of time from them because every minute is so precious. In the long run, I know that when we get back to Texas, my kids going to have an adjustment period and life will take a little longer to slip back into whatever normal is for our family. But for now, Mommy's going to give them their bedtime and whatever other time they want.

I've got three days left and it's not nearly long enough.

Totally Normal: Stressed the Hell Out
June 27, 2009

AS WE'RE GETTING READY to go, the normalcy of everything is striking. To include the urge to publicly spank my kid. Surely not, you must think. What kind of parent, leaving for another five months in a combat zone, loses her patience within the last twenty-four hours of getting ready to go?

Me.

Initially, the girls were being fine. Just laughing and having a good time. But then the touching and the grabbing and the I-wants kept going and going and going. They were like two little Energizer bunnies and it stopped being funny after we sat in Dick's Sporting Goods waiting for Daddy to pick out some fishing equipment (this takes longer than me in Saks on any day of the week, trust me on this one).

When they refused to stand still any longer, I was that crazy mom carrying one kid out of the store under my arm and pulling the other one behind her.

They say kids acting out prior to parents deploying is normal. I've also heard from other spouses that in the days before a deployment, the sniping and the bickering get to the point where both are relieved when the plane finally lifts off. The kids have both done something similar today and while at the moment, I would have been glad to get on a plane, that feeling only lasted about a second before the guilt started.

I told my husband that I felt bad for losing my patience with the kids. He said he understood but that it was more important for him to have fun before he left than to make them behave. Maybe he's on to something. Maybe he's not. But either way it goes, one of my precious fifteen days was spent arguing with my kids. I can't get this day back but tonight at bedtime, I talked to my girls and asked that we try to make tomorrow as good as possible before we left.

So we'll see how it goes. Wish me luck.

Going Back
Jun 29, 2009

I'M SITTING IN JFK, waiting for my ungodly long layover to be over. I've got internet and Starbucks (after an obscenely long wait and rude service) and I should be in a writer's paradise, right? I mean, after all, I haven't written anything on my WIP in two weeks and I've really only started thinking about my writing career the last few days to take my mind off leaving my kids once again.

So I should be thrilled, right? Peace and quiet. Chilling and writing?

Yeah, not so much.

My heart hurts. My youngest was up this morning at three when I was getting dressed (there was a lobster that was going to bite her) and she asked me to 'nuggle with her. Each time I thought she was asleep and I'd try to extricate myself from her embrace, she'd tighten her arms around my neck. It just about killed me. My oldest didn't wake up, but it was a close thing (you can hear a bug walking on Mom's floor).

Finally made it out of the house for my brother to take us to Bangor Airport (the troop greeters were there, which is awesome). Did fine until a little guy on our flight was screaming. Most passengers were upset because the kid was crying. It worked me over pretty good because all I could imagine was my daughters getting themselves all worked up looking for Mommy and Daddy today.

God, this sucks. I keep telling myself that it's worth it to give up a year of my life to provide for my kids and in eighteen years when my daughters have both of their college educations paid for that it will be worth it.

Right now, that's pretty cold comfort.

Settling Back In
July 3, 2009

IT'S BEEN A WEEK since I left my kiddos and I've got to say, settling in has been depressingly easy. It's as though the last two weeks of leave have been nothing but a blur. I wonder how the kids are doing. I've tried to call but Mom has been keeping them busy to keep their minds occupied, which is a good thing.

For myself, I slept a lot, trying to get back on the right time. Jet lag hasn't been nearly as bad for me as it has been for my husband, who's on day shift. But, if by jet lag, you mean the normal insomnia hasn't hit, then you'd be right. It's truly funny that I have more time for a shower and shaving my legs in Iraq than I do in the States. You wouldn't think that being a soldier takes less work than being a mom but in my case, it seems to be true.

Slipping back into the writing thing has been tougher than I thought it would be, until the internet went down and I was forced to stare at my computer screen. I put on some new tunes by a favorite band and dug into revisions and before I knew it, I'd crossed over the thousand-word threshold. Not a lot for me, but better than nothing considering I haven't written anything for the last month.

And the other exciting news I have to share is that I'm now part of the Mom's Writer Literary Magazine team. You might have seen the announcement on my website, but I'll be blogging with the gals over there as well. My first blog is due on 10 July, so I'll be sure to post a link to it then. In the meantime, I've got to come up with something profound to say in my column titled "Wearing Mommy's Combat Boots."

All in all, it's been all too easy to slip back into the routine. I guess I expected things to change but nothing has. We're still here. It's still hot and dirty and people are worried about the wrong things.

Business as usual, I guess.

Offensive?
July 7, 2009

RIGHT BEFORE I DEPLOYED, the Austin RWA asked me to speak. As a member, I figured everyone who might want to know something about Army life had already asked, but I said sure, why not.

I talked about being a woman in the Army. About the war. About leaving my kids. I really didn't think it was an offensive talk, just a little about how I see the world as a mom, as a soldier, and as a writer.

Someone, apparently was offended. It was mentioned on our loop that a guest was so offended by my talk that she refused to return to the meetings. I try to think back to what I could have said or done to offend anyone and I'm drawing a blank.

This is absolutely relevant to my life as a writer, and it's a lesson I'm struggling to learn from.

Right now, I'm sitting in Iraq, wondering what on earth I could have said that would upset someone so much that they would avoid the company of such a fantastic group of writers like the Austin RWA. And then I stopped.

Some people find the very idea of war and soldiering offensive. It could be that I was simply there, as a soldier, and the idea of me offended her. I don't know and the bottom line is that I'll never know. I can sit here and obsess or I can let it go (my writing about it is my attempt to let it go).

The lesson in here is that someone is not going to like what I've written. Someone will (hopefully not but I'm nothing if not a realist) be offended by the way I've written my books, my subject matter, or my attitude toward certain aspects of war. If I'm going to succeed as a writer, I can't pay attention to everyone who is offended by what I've written. I'm completely open to criticism and maybe if I knew what I'd said to irritate this person, I could reflect on it.

But the bottom line is that someone will find my portrayal of war and America's soldiers offensive. I wish it were otherwise but I can't fix that. This is my passion. The soldiers I live with and work with and have deployed with inspire the books I write. I can't change that and I don't know that I would.

So I won't apologize for my portrayals of American soldiers. We can respectfully agree to disagree but I won't apologize. And that, in and of itself, will probably be offensive to someone.

This is me and these are my books. And it's hopefully just the beginning of the story.

What I Really Want to Know
July 14, 2009

WHEN I SCREW UP, I think I'm pretty good at admitting it. That's part of being an officer that I remember from training my lieutenants as a young Staff Sergeant and Sergeant First Class. Own up. Your soldiers will respect you more and you'll sleep better at night.

So I can't help it if someone is too stupid to realize that they're too stupid for their current job. I know I'm being blunt, but come on, do you really expect anything less from me at this point?

So what I really, really want to know is why some people don't get fired? Is it their ability to keep six pounds of makeup from melting off their face in 112 degree heat? Why is it that the most incompetent people get to keep their jobs? We're seven months in at this point! Either you're going to learn your job or you're not. How many chances do people get?

And here's what really sets me off about the whole darn situation. If I screw up, my boss will go over my ass with a wire brush. And then pour alcohol on it. So why am I held to account when others aren't? Either hold us all to the same standard or there's no standard.

The argument I hear is, "well, they volunteer to be here and serve during war." I'd volunteer to be in the Infantry, but doesn't mean I belong there. Some jobs require technical skills that some people just won't master. Ever. So why continue to subject an entire brigade combat team to less than the best? Hell, I'll take mediocre at this point. Even lazy. I'm just really tired of incompetent.

New Adventures: Company Executive Officer
July 20, 2009

SO I'M NOW GOING to be my company XO. I go from being that lieutenant, you know the one with the big mouth and the attitude for days, to being that lieutenant, the most squared away one my commander has (which is total bullshit because I am a disaster on a good day).

But it's cool considering all the drama he and I went through when I got to the company. Let's just say that when you have more time in service than someone, it's really hard to take criticism from them. On any grounds. Even when they're right. But I stepped back and stopped taking things personally and now? Now he wants me to be the XO to make sure the upcoming change of command inventories go smoothly.

Which is cool. I'm reasonably certain I can handle it, but the platoon leaders aren't going to like it. Oh, because the days of the PLs sitting around and not being tasked to do anything? Yeah, those days are so over. They will learn about property accountability. They will learn about maintenance. They, not their soldiers, will brief maintenance issues. And they are going to have reports due.

Yeah, it's going to be a heck of a lot different for one of them, who has surfed to the end of the internet and shown ZERO initiative since, oh, I don't know, OCS. Nice guy. Useless officer. So we're going to see if we can't fix, rather than complain about, that problem.

All in all, I'm excited to be the XO. I get an office and I get to do a real job for the first time in a long time. Watch out.

Property Accountability Nightmare
July 24, 2009

CHANGE OF COMMAND IS never fun. Honestly, it's a huge pain in the ass but alas, it is also completely necessary. In our case, we're a signal company in a deployed brigade combat team. What this means is that we have a ton of equipment scattered all over northern Iraq.

The reason this is a problem is because we've got to account for it. The incoming commander must physically see every piece of equipment and no, he doesn't get a pass because we're at war. The other fun part of change of command is component hand receipts. Every screwdriver, every wrench must be accounted for. It's a major pain, made worse by the fact that component hand receipts haven't been maintained. So when I came on board to my platoon, it was like the equipment had existed in a void. Unfortunately for all parties involved, I managed to track down the issue hand receipts, which means that as of March of last year, the property book officer can now prove what was issued to the company. Which also means that someone is buying a whole lot of missing stuff.

The Army in general will only charge you for one month's base pay, unless negligence can be proven. I have no idea what the way forward is but I strongly suspect that multiple people are going to be losing some money.

Let me tell you what a good feeling it is to know that I will not be one of them. Why? Because I am a royal bitch when it comes to inventories. I demanded component hand receipts and if they didn't exist, I created them. My inventories took a month and then I signed it down to my section sergeants so that the only thing I physically owned was my laptop computers.

The bottom line is that when your paycheck is on the line, you have to be an ass about property. Hopefully, my platoon learned from my brief tenure as their PL and now knows what right looks like regarding property. I know I'm probably the only one not sweating the inventories, other than the fact that we will be sweating while doing them because it's hot as hell up here.

And that's my new life as the company XO.

What a Week
July 26, 2009

WELL, THE COMPANY HAS survived its first three days with me as XO. So far, I've managed to piss off the platoon sergeants and threaten to quit if my CO didn't support me.

What a great start.

Actually, it wasn't that bad. My good friend Arnie once pointed at me and said, "This is energy. Point her in a direction and something is going to happen. You may not like what occurs, but something will definitely take place." I loved that description of me, especially because if you know Arnie, he's the most analytical man I know. I loved working with Arnie because he forced me to slow down.

I don't have that here. Right now, I have a commander who's a little tense about his upcoming change of command and I have platoon sergeants who are mad because the XO isn't doing their jobs for them anymore. So I have all this energy (because let's face it, even as a platoon leader, I've been underutilized for the last year) and I'm going to put it to use. I'm going to get our supply system right and I'm going to train the new lieutenants we have in the company. One of them is really excited to be part of the team, the other one, I'm not so sure. But we'll get through it, one way or another. Four months to go until redeployment...

Oh No You Didn't
July 28, 2009

I HAVE DECIDED THAT I'm not overly approachable. Which isn't really a surprise at this point in my life.

I'm generally shaping up to be one mean bitch of an officer. The other day, I had a Second Lieutenant decide to task someone in my platoon. He did not speak to that platoon sergeant. He did not speak to me. He claims to have spoken to the CO but the CO did not clear it either. When I sent him a gentle reminder that, hey, you really shouldn't just announce these things at meetings, but should coordinate with one of us first, he sent me back this shitty little reply that he'd spoken with someone else (not in any way shape or form in my NCO's food chain).

So I ripped his head off. I explained to said Second Lieutenant that he was missing the point and that for future reference, if he wishes to task my soldiers he will speak with me first. I was not nice about it, especially since this guy is supposedly prior service and should know better. I wouldn't tolerate that from any of my peers and I'm damn sure not going to tolerate it because this guy is afraid to talk to me.

Some people are not cut out for the Army. I'm of the mindset that if you want to be in the Army, first off, it's a privilege, not a right. Second, you better get some thick skin and grow a pair because we are a war time Army. We do not have the time nor the disposition to listen to someone whine about having their feelings hurt. Maybe it's just me but if you task someone, you task them through their leadership. I'm just pointing that out. And I've been bad about this in the past too and when corrected, I made sure I didn't do it again.

It was meant to be a teaching point, not an ass chewing, but unfortunately, it turned into an ass chewing. So we'll see what tomorrow brings.

The Best Book This Year
August 3, 2009

I WAS CRAVING A book that had a real emotional impact. I wanted some characters that I could care about, that I would cheer for and truly be happy for when the end came for them. Never in my wildest dreams did I think I'd find it in an author I hadn't read since I was a teenager.

You'll recall a couple of weeks ago, I posted about how Laura Kinsale was cool enough to fire me off a sample chapter of her new book, Lessons in French. I thought it was pretty neat, considering that (a). she's quite possibly the best romance writer out there and (b). I've been a fan of hers for years. One of the few books I've held on to over my many PCS moves has been The Shadow and the Star.

Somehow, I'd never read Seize the Fire and, as I'd fallen away from historical romances in general as I moved from adolescence into adulthood, I'd set her books on my shelf. But when my idea sparked for my next book delving into PTSD, I thought that I needed to go back to the true master of tortured heroes. I'd originally planned on My Sweet Folly but discovered that Seize the Fire was truly about a tortured war hero.

It takes a lot to make me cry. I haven't cried at the end of a fiction book in years. But when I finished Seize the Fire, I felt this incredible sigh, this powerful emotion. She wrote it years ago, when Vietnam was still a fresh wound on our nation's veterans. There were still Vietnam Vets in the Army back then.

Ms. Kinsale wrote an absolutely amazing story. I'm grateful that she did not trivialize what her hero had done and that the heroine loved him regardless. I only hope that all of our returning heroes somehow find the same love and acceptance from their families and our society when the war is but a distant memory.

Assumptions
August 4, 2009

YOU KNOW WHAT THEY say about "assume," right? It's a cliché simply because it's one of those truths that you can't ever really escape. But what if assumptions are more than that? What if they're a bigger problem than you realize?

I assume. I assume a lot. As an officer with fourteen years in service, twelve of them enlisted, I assume that anyone who's been in the Army for a minute has had similar experiences to mine. At least on the things that should be basic knowledge, such as property accountability and soldier issues. But I find myself more and more frustrated and after talking it over with a mentor of mine, I realize that the problem isn't necessarily with them, but with my assumptions.

See, I assume that as an SFC, you would have accomplishing the mission and the welfare of your soldiers foremost in your mind. I assume that as an SFC, some things should not have to be spelled out. I assume that you understand that there are such things as implied tasks that go along with accomplishing the mission. And I assume that when an officer gives you an order, you absolutely use that as the basis for accomplishing the mission.

I do not assume that as a senior NCO or officer you have zero knowledge of what right looks like regarding property accountability. I do not assume that I must break every single task down to the minutiae and I assume that you know what minutiae means. I do not assume that making a simple correction is going to send you on a diatribe about people freaking out over property.

There is a reason that I am frustrated with some of the leadership in my company. I believe now that the problem lies with me. I assume standards of conduct are the norm, when in fact, watching TV and chilling out are. I assume that checking on your subscribers is a norm when, instead, the norm is to let the system fail and only then maybe get off your ass to fix it. I assume that when I say to do something tonight, that means it happens tonight, not that as long as it happens by morning, it's okay.

So I think the problem is that I assume.

This actually has relevance in my writing. I write about military life and I make assumptions about what my reader knows. I assume that someone knows that a brigade combat team is made up of battalions. I assume that people know the difference between officers and NCOs and that they know what NCO stands for. I assume that when I talk about the responsibilities of command, that people know that I'm talking about an officer's responsibilities and not an enlisted soldier's responsibilities.

These assumptions have the potential to derail my writing. If I leave out explanations, I risk pulling the reader out of the story to go look things up. If I put in too much, I risk patronizing or talking down to them. So the importance is to find the right balance and create my world without pages of explanation.

Will I be able to paint my world here in Iraq, as the XO, and make my platoon sergeants and platoon leaders understand what I expect without having to waste precious time and resources explaining every detail?

We shall see.

Today I...
August 5, 2009

...WAS TOLD THAT I am too abrasive and not gentle enough when I deal with people. That I am going around backstabbing people and that I am not going to succeed in this organization. When I

responded that I know I'm aggressive, I was asked
how has that worked out for me?

I stated that for fourteen years, it's worked out
pretty damn good so far. What a way to start the
day, huh?

Vietnam Help
August 6, 2009

OKAY, SO I NEED help. I'm starting a new book
and I really want to tie in PTSD from Vietnam to
my new character home from Iraq, who is seriously
screwed up. I'm hoping you'll take a look and email
me with answers, impressions, or anything else you
think I might be able to use.

I guess the first thing I'm looking to know is who
did you know that went over there? What was it like
when they came home? How bad was the anti-
soldier sentiment? What did these guys do when
they came home? How were they different? What did
they say? Did they talk about it? Were there any
significant events that started people changing the
way we as a society looked at our soldiers? Basically,
when was the turnaround from baby killer to hero?
How did you feel when you watched the news? How
is the media coverage different today than back then
about the war?

Seems like that should be a good starting point.
And I know you, you're going to rally the troops and
get me all kinds of information. I want this to be
personal observations, not like Wikipedia entries...

Does that make sense? Any and all help will be greatly appreciated.

My Latest Project
August 8, 2009

WELL, IN ORDER TO stop focusing on all the things in my unit that I have no influence to change and that really piss me off, I'm starting a new book. Actually, I'd written the first few pages about a week ago when I had the start of the idea that will eventually form into the new project but I threw most of that out as it wasn't quite right.

What's really interesting about this book is the research that's going into it. I have to learn a ton about how the mind works and the different aspects of PTSD other than nightmares.

And I've chosen to make this book a comparison between the Iraq war and Vietnam. I find it amazing that when I talk to Vietnam Vets, their stories are remarkably similar regarding the anti-war sentiment. I spoke with one of the majors today whose father was in Vietnam and he made an interesting statement.

The major said that soldiers are still regarded with contempt. He was very blunt when he said that people pay lip service to the "soldier as hero" but when it comes right down to it, soldiers will still be condemned for the actions they are expected to do in order to come back home.

His thoughts and the thoughts of other Vets who've already talked with me really got me thinking about our society. About what's really important. My mom told me that during Nam, the nightly news was about the body count. Every night was the latest news from Nam. A retired Air Force colonel told me that when she was in Vietnam, the protests were surreal and far away from the realities of the war. Different people, different places, and different perspectives.

I find it interesting that an active duty officer would say that the people who praise the soldiers aren't really supportive. I find it interesting that some civilians who support the troops would never send their children into the military. And most interesting is the perception that if you can't find anything else to do, join the military. It's perceived as only an option for people who have no other prospects in life. Hell, that's how I got here, and it was the best decision I ever made.

So learning about my parents' generation and my parents' war is very interesting so far. The soundtrack to my WIP is all classic rock, despite working on a contemporary novel. We'll see where it goes.

I just hope that the people who've helped me so far and continue to offer guidance will enjoy the final product.

The Latest from the Front
August 11, 2009

IT'S A CLICHÉ TO say "Fool me once, shame on you; fool me twice, shame on me." It's a cliché because it's true. I've had several run-ins with a certain individual who's your best friend one week and treats you like a piece of shit next week when you're not properly deferential.

I am so tired of it. If you want a relationship to be completely professional, act like it. Don't play games. Counsel me on specific failings. I have them. But don't tell me I'm a backstabber without calling me on a specific incident. And don't undermine me because I was trying to do the right thing when you refused to do the right thing despite being told repeatedly to do so.

I screw up. All the time, in fact. But some things are supposed to be important and some things you're not supposed to take shortcuts on. You should not be able to sleep at night knowing that you've made your soldier sign for equipment that they do not have. How is that good leadership? How is that teaching the young soldier what right looks like? And I expect to be called on things when I am told to execute and I fail to.

But don't expect me to read your mind and don't expect me to kiss your ass. Decide from the moment you meet me: do you want the truth or not? If not, tell me that and I shall endeavor to remain silent (which is a little bit of a stretch but I'll at least give it a whirl). Don't get mad when I tell you that you have a problem.

Don't accept what I tell you as truth. Know whether or not I'm right. I make mistakes. Don't get mad at me if I do make mistakes when you do nothing to teach me what's right, oh ye of greater rank. Just because you outrank me doesn't mean shit in my book.

I think ultimately two things are going on. One, I'm tired of being the asshole. Why do I feel like I'm the only one who cares about the bigger picture? My company exists to support the brigade. Why don't we act like it? And two, I'm frustrated with the people around me who still have jobs who should have been fired. They should have been moved and ultimately, I feel like I'm being held to a different standard than the people around me. It is difficult to maintain a motivated spirit in that kind of environment.

But, I'm going to drive on. I'm holding my breath until certain personnel change out around here. And I'm beyond ready to come home. It's time. A year is too damn long, no matter how you shake it. Just too long.

I Have Failed
August 13, 2009

FOR THOSE OF YOU not familiar with Army life, the following might appear somewhat strange. For those of you who know me, please tell me what I can do to fix this situation.

I chose the easy wrong over the hard right. I failed my platoon and my company. I can excuse it all day long but at the end of the day, the responsibility is mine.

I tried to have a certain subordinate (we'll call this person Subordinate A) fired. I failed. This person still has a job and the entire brigade suffers because Subordinate A has a critical job that Subordinate A is incapable of doing. In order to be successful Subordinate A needs to go back to school and learn the skills for the job that is required of Subordinate A's position.

I was moved from that job to my current job, where I worked with Subordinate B. I did counsel Subordinate B but I deliberately chose not to address certain failings because I felt that I did not have the support of the chain of command. After failing to get Subordinate A fired, the last thing I would be able to do would be to fire Subordinate B. Accepting that I had to work with Subordinate B allowed me to go to work each day and put on a happy face and pretend that everything was okay, peachy even, despite having significant misgivings about Subordinate B's lack in capabilities and work ethic.

I let these misgivings go in order to keep the peace. I found work-arounds that kept the peace in order to make the mission happen. I let things slide that I should have corrected and at the end of it all, the situation has exploded in my face. Subordinate B was completely disrespectful toward me in a situation where I was attempting to conduct officer professional development. When I went to my chain of command, I was told that I was not doing enough to communicate with this person. I took the comments from my chain of command to mean that they laid the blame for this situation at my feet because I am particularly grating and not at Subordinate B's because he's "one of the boys".

My chain of command is only partially correct. Because I failed to inform them when I was truly having problems and to clearly communicate what those problems were, when the situation reached critical mass, I was left holding the bag of blame. It is easier to blame me than to look honestly at the people around them and say perhaps there is an issue.

So I failed. I looked at the situation I was in and thought, how would this look to me? I assessed that because I was the common denominator, then anyone looking at problems between either Subordinate A and Subordinate B and myself would focus on me as the source of the problem.

I assumed that had I gone to the chain of command, they would have blamed me anyway. Which is ultimately what happened.

So now I don't know how to find my way out of this. My chain of command has formally reprimanded me for my part in the problem and I accept that I have responsibility for creating this situation. My commander despises me and treats me like I'm something he stepped in.

I have failed and I don't know how to fix it, if I even can.

Thanks for the Feedback
August 14, 2009

WELL WITH ALL THE drama that's been ongoing in my life, I've neglected to say thank you for all the wonderful feedback that everyone offered on the new project. Your comments and reactions were greatly appreciated and thank you very much for your candor.

Along the writing news, I finally received my Golden Heart results today and while I did not final in the widely respected contest, I actually came pretty close with one of my books, so that was exciting in and of itself.

I'll say this and I've said it before. Writing has most certainly kept me sane over here and I'm not sure where I'd be without having it as a means to get my frustrations out. I've had one hell of a bunch of inspiration, that's for sure, so here's hoping the well doesn't run dry anytime soon.

Later!

Submitting, The Comments
August 21, 2009

THANK YOU EVERYONE WHO emailed and commented on what they've done during the submission process. It's been a tremendous learning experience for me just gaining perspective from people who've been there and are there now.

The single biggest agreement about the submission process, regardless of whether it's for editors or agents, is the waiting. For unpublished writers, the wait can be months, if not longer. I had a rejection from an agency a year and a half after I'd submitted to them but I adhere to the ninety-day rule. If I hadn't heard from an agent after about three months, I assumed there was no interest. The fun part about email queries is that you don't necessarily get a response. Agents Janet Reid and Jessica Faust have both commented on their blogs how nasty exchanges get sometimes when an email rejection is sent. As a result, many agents simply don't respond, which leaves the budding writer in a near constant limbo.

The next hardest part about submitting, again with wide agreement, is the rejections. Both silence and "it's just not right for me" blanket rejections offer little incentive to the writer to keep going. As the writer progresses, however, usually rejections may get a little more informative and sometimes, the best answers are rejections with suggestions for improvements as well as an invitation to resubmit. Those rejections give the unpublished writer the opportunity to revisit the manuscript with comments in mind for specific issues and ultimately, can help the writer grow.

For many writers, the ultimate challenge is what to do during the wait. Many mentioned working on the next project because, for a writer, there is always work to be done. Either copy edits, galleys, proofs or simply starting the next book. Keeping busy is a way to keep from obsessively waiting for the phone to ring or the inbox to chime, plus it helps advance your career as well.

Choosing writing as a career is not for the faint‑hearted. I truly thought in December 2007 when I'd written "The End" that I'd created a masterpiece. Said "masterpiece" is in the trash now, though the heart of that idea has been retained in another story. Stay busy, stay after it, and above all, keep writing. It only takes one yes to move you from hobbyist to professional.

First Day of School
August 28, 2009

TODAY MY OLDEST DAUGHTER starts kindergarten. Because she's staying with my mom, my oldest will be going to the same school I went to as a little girl. I remember my first day of school. I wore a little green windbreaker and a sticker with my name on it. I was scared getting on the bus that first day. But I had my mom there, holding my hand and taking pictures and making it into a big adventure for me. My mom is there again, being there because I can't.

The hardest thing about being gone is that my daughter will remember this. She'll remember us not being there and she'll remember my mom being there. Which is really great, because she'll have a closeness with my mom that I never imagined possible with us being dual military. I'll remember the day through pictures.

I'm sad about not being there. This is a pretty big milestone for my little girl. Just one more thing that as a military mom, I miss out on. We can talk about sacrifice all day long but at the end of the day, it's personal. It's about missed birthdays and weddings. It's about missed first days of school. It's about time. I'll never get this day back. I'll remember it through this blog post and the pictures my mom sends and the phone call tonight to hear all about it. But today is gone.

I can only make the rest of the days count. I made the choice to be in the Army and have a family. Doesn't make the consequences of that choice easier to deal with. I'll probably find a way to write about this someday, down the road. When it's a little less fresh and a little less raw.

I hope today is a happy one for my daughter. She's going to school with her cousin, also something I never imagined she'd get to do because of our military lives. I'm looking forward to the pictures and hearing her tell us about it.

Most of all, I'm looking forward to being home. To taking her to school myself and meeting her teachers and helping her with her homework. Because those are the days I've got to look forward to.

Looking back doesn't accomplish anything but regret. And regret will spoil those days still to come.

So as you're walking your kids to school today or sending them off on the school bus, remember there are thousands of moms who aren't there today to do the same. There are thousands of dads who are expected to act like today is just another day. Enjoy the little things.

They really are what's important.

Through Fresh Eyes
August 29, 2009

WELL, WE HAD A change of command and there's a new tone in my world. No longer do I feel cornered, like I'm one screw up away from being fired. I feel empowered, relieved, and excited that we've got a new command team that will work toward making the brigade better as a whole.

As much time as I spent frustrated over the last few months, I have learned a lot, about myself and about understanding other people's limitations. As an example, I think my brain goes a little bit too fast. I was the narrator for the change of command ceremony today and my CSM told me to slow down. I read so slow, I felt like I sounded like I was screwing around, talking on slow motion. But apparently, it was perfect for the ceremony. It felt weird. Really weird.

It taught me that just because I see the world one way and understand things that seem very simple to me, it doesn't mean that someone else has the same understanding. I need to slow down when I talk to people.

I see the same problem in my writing as I'm revising. I'll write something that makes perfect sense to me but then when I go back and look at it, the words make absolutely no sense. I've discovered that simpler ideas per sentence are easier to communicate, so even though I talk in run-on sentences and fragments, my writing should not hold the same.

Over the last few months, I learned how truly easy it is to make a difference, for good or for bad. I've learned about my own personal limitations and I've tried to apply those to my writing life, stretching beyond what I'd thought I was capable of. I've had some fantastic mentors, both military and literary and I've truly benefited from both. On the Army side, I've had good friends of mine willing to kick me in the ass and tell me to straighten up. It's so much easier to hear, "hey, you're screwing up" from someone you respect and admire than someone you despise. It's the same thing with writing. I found a critique partner (through sheer luck!) who was willing to tell me, "hey, this needs work now let's get after it."

If either of those folks had let me slide, I would not have grown, either as a leader or as a writer. Find someone in your writing life who cares enough to tell you this isn't as good as it can be. Be that person for someone else. Don't be mean and say this sucks. But be honest and offer suggestions on how to improve.

You'll find you benefit more than you realize.

Fresh Start Part 2
August 30, 2009

WRITING IS A CHALLENGE. It is so much more than simply putting words on paper. It's making those words into a coherent story that people care about.

Why on earth would I write, when I'm a fulltime mom, fulltime Army officer and fulltime wife, housekeeper, veterinarian (all of our pets are another story)? Why would I add one more thing to my already full plate?

I write because I have to. Because at the end of the day, the stories are in my head and this is something that I can do down the road for years to come.

Coming to Iraq has impacted my writing. Foremost being that I've had more time to write this year than I'll probably ever have again. I've used that time wisely (I hope) by practicing my craft daily. This has enabled me to develop certain practices, such as writing every day or editing my stuff in Word rather than Scrivener, where I write. Of the year I spent here, I can honestly say that there was only about a month total where I did not write every single day.

I refuse to believe that I won't sell. For me, it's a matter of when, not if. While that may be wishful thinking, I choose to look at it as positive thinking.

I have a new company commander now and it feels like that fresh start when I first start a new project. Clean slate, able to do what needs to get done to tell the story. There will inevitably be rough periods, just like the process of writing a new book, when I step back and try to figure out what the heck happened to get me where I am right now. But that is all part of the process.

I've felt smothered in my professional capacity during the last few months. This was in part due to my own stubbornness and feeling that I knew what right was supposed to be, but also due to lack of communication and a lack of a willingness to communicate. Writing is communication between me and my characters. When I don't listen to what they're telling me, I stagnate. When I'm not willing to push the boundaries and challenge them, the story stagnates.

So here's to new beginnings and fresh starts. In writing and in life!

Failure to Communicate
September 2, 2009

IN THE PAST FEW weeks, there have been a multitude of problems in my company and the more I reflect, there was a single source of failure: inability to communicate. I stopped talking to my platoon sergeant, my commander stopped talking to me, and all in all, personalities got in the way.

You wouldn't think that this would be a problem in the Army, but we're an organization of people and we all have our own failings. Since the new command has taken over, several changes have occurred. One, we're all communicating. We're talking to our brigade staff section counterparts; we're talking to each other. We're simply giving updates to keep everyone on the same page.

All because we started talking again.

As a writer, it's easy to look at a character and say, "oh, just talk to so and so and the problem will go away." Unfortunately, talking in real life is significantly more difficult than it is on the page. So many problems in novels are chalked up to failure to communicate and dismissed as too easy to have fixed. What I think readers and writers fail to realize is that failure to communicate is often the heart of most problems but we tend to write it as a simple solution.

It's hard to talk to people, especially when there are hurt feelings and bruised egos and wounded pride in the mix. It's really difficult to look someone in the eye and say, "this is where I think you screwed up." So why do we dismiss it on the page?

In part, as the writer, it's too easy to have our characters say and do what we want them to do, so we have to create extraordinary situations to keep our hero and heroine apart. This is great for Romantic Suspense but what about those of us who don't write R/S? One of the things I struggled with was how to keep my hero and heroine at odds without someone threatening the situation?

That was when I discovered that the problem between my characters was a failure to communicate. It's easy to sit back and say "husband, talk to wife. Tell her what happened to you while you were at war." I'll confess to wishing my own husband talked more about what he experienced, but I also recognize that me nagging him to talk would have the opposite reaction. So when he does choose to talk about it, I listen. I don't judge him. I simply shut my mouth (a monumental task, trust me) and listen.

It's difficult to understand how someone who talks as much as I do can have such a hard time communicating. But today when my former platoon sergeant came and asked me for advice, I listened. I offered feedback, using where he and I failed as a team as a teaching point for him. In my writing, I've got a character who refuses to acknowledge that he's got a problem and his wife refuses to wait any longer for him to come around.

Both situations were a failure to communicate. My old platoon sergeant and I worked through a lot of issues this morning, but it took both of us stepping away from the other for a really long period of time before either of us was able to discuss on a professional level what happened. In my WIP, I don't have the luxury of letting my hero take time to figure out what's wrong—he has to do it now or my readers will lose interest. So I have to add urgency to his learning how to communicate, which is as difficult as getting an alcoholic to admit he has a problem.

I learn more about my characters every day as I interact with the people around me and at least attempt to be a good communicator. As I continue on my journey as a writer and a leader, I only hope to share my experiences and help someone else learn through my mistakes.

Are We Unfair to Heroines or Just Women?
September 7, 2009

SO HERE'S SOMETHING I bet you'll never see coming. There are people over here who I can't stand. In my previous position, I had two key leaders, both females, who were unable to perform their duties. One of those individuals told anyone who would listen that I simply didn't like her and that I was targeting her and "being mean." Yes those words were used (we're in the Army, people, but that's another discussion).

Anyway, both individuals retained their jobs, despite their complete incompetence, and despite the fact that their failure to perform negatively impacted an entire brigade's ability to communicate. When I look at the situation, I see two soldiers who failed to perform. What my seniors see is that they've got a female being mean to two other females.

Are you kidding me? I wish.

How on earth does this relate to writing? It's actually exceptionally applicable because guess who gets blamed for almost all wrongs in a romance novel? If you said the heroine, you'd be right on the money. So here's my issue: If as a female officer, I am harder on other female soldiers, regardless of rank, does that impact how I view female characters in movies and books? Absolutely. The other interesting fact is that when women critique other people's writing, they are harder on female authors than they are on male authors.

So what do we do about it? In real life, should we be 'nicer' to other women simply because our male counterparts refuse to hold them to the same standard that they hold men to? Should we cut our heroines some slack because maybe we can't really say how we'd react in the same situation or maybe because she does something we completely wouldn't do in the same situation?

I think it should be a little bit of both. Maybe, in real life, we should spend more time developing our fellow women. In both instances, I attempted to, but was overcome by events. Not an excuse, a fact. Then both people stopped working for me, limiting my influence even further. Conversely, a wonderful example of women supporting and mentoring others is my home RWA chapter in Austin. All one has to do is post a question and folks will be jumping up with the answer and trying to help. There are wonderful mentors in the group, all willing to offer advice from how they got through a similar situation.

In writing, all I can do is identify what drives my heroine and have her act true to her character. With any kind of luck, I'll have portrayed the emotional stakes correctly so my readers will understand where she's coming from.

The real world is always more difficult to get right than fiction. In fiction, I control what my characters do. But if I take too much control, I risk mixing up my heroine's motivation and that, more than anything, will have readers throwing books at the walls.

A Visceral Response
September 9, 2009

AS A MOM, NOTHING pushes my freak out button faster than a crying baby. I don't know what it is but a crying baby triggers my mom reflex to where I need to pick it up and try to soothe it. This is a gut reaction that is seriously intense for me. Today at the gym, there was some movie on about a concentration camp in WWII. There was a baby that people were trying to hide from the guards. I was nearly in tears before I asked the gym personnel to change the channel.

Why such a strong reaction to a movie?

I think in part, it has to do with being away from my own kids. Knowing that there are times when my daughters are upset and I'm thousands of miles away is incredibly frustrating. It's hard not being able to hold my kids. So there was that. Combine that emotion with the emotion of being unable to protect my kids which was triggered by the movie and we've got a recipe for a strong emotional reaction.

What's this got to do with writing?

As a writer, I want to inspire strong reactions in my readers. I want them to care deeply about my characters to the point that when they laugh, my reader laughs. When my characters are hurting, I want my reader to hurt. So as a writer, this reaction I had intrigued me. Being able to analyze where the emotions come from will enable me in the future to pull from that emotional base and put it on paper.

If I've inspired a strong reaction in my readers, I will have connected with them in a way that all writers dream of. How often have you read a book where you just don't care about the characters? Finding a way to connect deeply with your readers is a challenge for every writer.

So the next time you have a strong reaction to something, sit back and try to figure out why. The answers might surprise you, and it's something you can put in your writers' rucksack for future use.

Top Ten Things Not Overheard When Talking About LT Jess
September 10, 2009

10. SHE'S A PEOPLE person.

9. Her children must be so polite and well-mannered.

8. You have to guess what she's thinking.

7. Her body language is confusing, I can't tell if she's angry or happy.

6. She's so cute and flirty.

5. She really doesn't get her point across well.

4. She's too much of a girly-girl to be in the Army.

3. She doesn't tell me when I'm screwing up;, she's kind of vague and indirect.

2. She's so polite, she never swears or loses her temper.

1. She's so nice.

That is all...

Writer's Block
September 14, 2009

I HAVE A CYCLE of writing. Not a process like other authors talk about. Mine's a cycle. I go through bursts of being able to knock out three, four, even five thousand words in a very short amount of time. It feels great to look back over my word-count log and see the progress I make. Then there are other days when I'm absolutely stuck and can't get to the next sentence, let alone move the story forward. For me, these days are beyond frustrating because I know I'm capable of so much more. It's irritating because as much as I have to write 2000 words per day to accomplish my daily target, on these days, I'm lucky to scratch out a thousand. These days usually only last a day or so. But lately, I've been stuck. I'm sure it's not a lack of motivation, as I'm pretty damned excited that my agent has me on the submissions schedule for this month. If anything should be motivating at this point, that should be (of course, you're talking about the girl who still gets goose-bumps when she thinks she even has an agent but that's another story). So what gives? I think, more than anything, I'm tired.

At the end of the night, I've been going for 12-15 hours. I'm simply tired. I have to make time for physical activity, as my weight is a nearly constant challenge. I find myself frustrated that I can barely knock out 2000 words when in days past I was able to write so much more. This is a reality that I will simply have to accept: I have a real job and real responsibilities. I can't sit and write fifty pages in a day until after I retire. So fatigue is part of it.

Another part of it is that I'm just in that slump that I have in every project. Right about the 50,000-word mark, I usually hit a what-the-heck-happens-next slump that I struggle through.

In this case, this slump happened to coincide with regular fatigue, exacerbating the problem. Inevitably, I'll pull out of it. I'll get a burst of energy or a spark of renewed vigor and my work pace will take off again. So I won't panic about the writer's block until I go weeks and weeks without writing. Then it will be time for a major reassessment. For now, I think it's time for a nap.

Jessica Scott

Describing the Rain
September 19, 2009

UNTIL YOU'VE LIVED IN the desert, you can't really appreciate the little things. Last night, I was lying in bed and there was a rumbling in the distance. Rumblings over here in Iraq are usually a bad thing but I lay there and listened. Then the sweetest sound filled the little metal connex that is my living quarters. Rain started tapping on the roof, first a few drops and then a downpour. It only lasted a few minutes but the sound, the beautiful sound of rain hitting the roof, was pure heaven.

This morning when I walked outside, there was moisture in the air. The smell was instantly reminiscent of any morning back in the States after a nighttime deluge. The ground was wet, the air cool and crisp like Fall. For a moment, I simply stood and breathed in the smell of something other than dirty, dusty air. Too often, we as writers get bogged down in describing a scene.

For me, most of my readers will never have been to Fort Hood, so I find myself describing things and places that I take for granted. I get lost in the detail and on the reread, my CP always asks me: what's important here? What does my reader need to know to anchor her in the scene? So just like this morning, when the smell of the rain was what I focused on, when I'm writing, I try to focus on the highlights. What's the overwhelming sensation you'll have in a bakery? Homemade scents. What about a flower shop? Bursts of color.

115

When you're describing a scene, don't tell me about the shrubs unless it's part of a bigger picture. Give me enough detail to anchor me there but not too much that I'd be skipping ahead to find out what happens next. But what was unique about the homemade scents in a bakery? Nothing. The reader expects it. What if you focused on the sounds of cooking? The clanging of pans from the back? Something different, right? Learn to describe the smell of the rain. The sound of it. Your reader expects you to tell her it's wet.

Where Do I Fit?
September 21, 2009

WHEN I SAY MILITARY romance, what do you think? I think a romance with military or former-military characters. Apparently, when I say military romance, agents and editors are thinking something else. They're thinking Romantic Suspense. Recently, I had a fantastic conversation with a fantastic Romantic Suspense author about where my book fits in the market. When she read it, she was reading it like it was a romantic suspense, but when I explained that it's straight romance, she said it changed the way she looked at it.

What does this have to do with anything? It's got to do with knowing where you fit. Which apparently failed to do prior to sending my stuff out to the broader writing world.

When I was pitching my books to agents, I was pitching with something to the effect of Suzanne

Jessica Scott

Brockmann has written blah blah blah. So what I was doing was gearing agents up for reading this like it was a Suzanne Brockmann when in fact I write nothing like Suzanne Brockmann.

I don't write R/S. In fact, I suck at it. Which means that when agents were looking at my stuff, they were expecting to see Suz and instead they saw what I was putting out there: straight romance.

It's no wonder I was soundly rejected. So the lesson here is do your market research. What I discovered in my conversation with Roxanne St. Claire was that there really isn't a whole lot out there like my stuff, which can be really good, but if I pitch saying that I'm like so-and-so, I better make sure I'm sending the right message. Otherwise, it's really bad.

So learn from this. Figure out where you fit in the market and be able to articulate that. Otherwise, you might be like me, banging my head against the wall.

The Spots on Your Point of View
September 22, 2009

I READ A FASCINATING article today in Psychology Today regarding perceptions of self. This article, "Mixed Signals" by Sam Gosling, pointed out that there are four categories of how we see ourselves.

"Bright Spots are things known by you and by others," like political affiliation and whether you're introverted or extroverted.

"Dark Spots are known neither by you nor others." These things are deeply subconscious influences that provide unknown sources of motivations and behaviors.

"Personal spots are known only by you," such as how you feel about your job—no really feel—or personal phobias.

"Blind Spots are things known only by others." These are the signals you send out in the world and have no idea that this is how others see you.

This article was absolutely intriguing on two levels for me, both as a leader and as a writer. As a leader, the Army teaches me that I must know myself. As a writer, I must know my characters. But according to Mr. Gosling, there's no way that I can truly know either one. On the one hand, it might be easier for me to know my characters because I'm creating them, but is it truly easy for me to write a heroine who sees the hero as a flatulent douchebag when he sees himself as a sensitive lover?

One way to use this information is to look at how your heroine does see the hero and vice versa. Many of the opening conflicts in romance novels start out because of miscommunication in exactly how the hero and heroine see the other person. Once they discover the true nature—the 'personal spots' as it were of the other person, then room for true love takes off.

This is a little too easy for me though, because in real life, it is nearly impossible for people to look at the negative aspects of themselves. So if you're going to write realistic characters, you have to find a way around the self-delusion that a person maintains. For instance, there is a key leader in my company who honestly thinks he's the best NCO in the company and that he's looked up to and admired. He's completely self-deluded because the soldiers hate him, don't respect him, and think he's a flatulence filled douchebag.

Why the disconnect? Because of the lies we tell ourselves. In my case, when my commander sat me down and told me that I was unapproachable, cold, not nice, and too aggressive, I wasn't surprised at all. For me, that was a sign that at least I wasn't feeding myself a load of bullshit that I was some nice and kind mommy figure. He seemed surprised, though, that I was not surprised by his assessment of me.

In writing, I struggle with having my characters not having the same lack of self-delusion. Right now, I've got a character who honestly believes he needs to be deployed because that's his entire purpose in life. He doesn't realize that he's staying deployed out of a deep-seated guilt for what happened to him and his wife doesn't know the reasons, either. Hence, their marriage is struggling. The major turning point in the story is going to be when he realizes how deep the level of self-delusion has really been and the consequences his self-delusion has had, both on him as a soldier and as a husband.

Mr. Gosling offers tools to help people look at how the world sees themselves. There are apps on Facebook called the Honesty Box and the You Just Get Me app, both of which are designed to help people see themselves how others see them. While you may never understand your dark spots, you may get a glimpse at the blind spots in your life.

As a writer, when you're developing your characters, draw a box and label it with the four categories. See if you can fill them out. You may get key insights into your characters before you get 200 pages into a manuscript and realize you have no idea what your character's motivation is.

The Mommy Box
September 24, 2009

MY DAUGHTER TURNS 5 today. I wasn't going to write about it because I'm taking it harder than I thought I was going to. You see, in order to be in Iraq and essentially give up on being a parent for a year, I've had to compartmentalize. I take all of my mommy stuff, my emotions, my thinking about my kids, anything at all that reminds me how bad it sucks to be in Iraq missing everything like my kid's first day at school, birthdays, and every other milestone (though I've got to say, I'm glad my mom is dealing with my youngest's potty training issues—thanks, Mom!), and put it all in a Mommy Box. I turn off the feelings and put them away. I don't think about it. I stay busy. I try not to talk about my family with anyone other than my husband, because at the end of the day, I just don't want to talk about it.

But my Mommy Box has cracked open several times this year with mixed results. My fun little panic attack episode back when the swine flu first broke and I had just read The Shack was one example (seriously, reading about a guy whose kid is murdered? Not good reading material for a mom who's separated from her kids by oceans and deserts but that's another post). Another was my daughter's first day of school. I bawled like a baby and was pretty down the next day, too. All until I was able to move my mind to something else and put the lid back on my Mommy Box.

For those of you who've never left your families behind, you might be wondering how I can do it. It's not a matter of how, it's a matter of necessity. I have to stay busy or the sadness will eat away at me. When I talk to the kids, I try to make them laugh (I'm not very good at it but I try).

My oldest told me the other day on the phone that she wanted to be an author like me. I asked her if she wanted to write stories with me when I get home. We started talking about her story where a kitten and a unicorn (I just typed uniform instead— think my fingers have muscle memory, much?) were playing tag. When I said the winner didn't have to take a nap, she thought it was the funniest thing in the whole world. It felt good to have something to share, even with the distance and the space between us.

My mom sent me a bunch of her artwork from school. On one of them was a note from her teacher. It said "I like how you put your name on your piece—that's what writers do." So not only does my kiddo want to be a writer (and I have to say, the secret part of me is thrilled that my kid looks up to me) but she's got the courage to tell people she's going to be a writer.

I hid my writing for the most part until I joined the Austin RWA. I still tend not to tell folks that I'm seeking publication. But my five year old has the courage to announce it to the world both that her mommy is a writer and that she wants to be like her mommy.

And that, folks, is worth any sacrifice.

Happy Birthday, baby. Mommy and Daddy will be home soon.

Refilling the Well
September 25, 2009

YOU'VE HEARD OF THIS before. LTC Grossman mentions it in the groundbreaking books On Killing and On Combat. He states flat out that you can go back to the well as much as you need to but if you don't take care of yourself, when you need it, the well will be dry. You'll have nothing to pull from when the poo and the fan have made babies and you're in a bad spot. It's critical for our soldiers to get enough rest, to eat well, and stay hydrated.

Spiritual fitness comes into this as well and that means taking a break from it all and being able to reset and recharge. R&R from Iraq is mandatory for ALL personnel, including the generals who make major decisions on US operations around the globe. It needs to be. For we as soldiers have a tendency to keep going until we collapse, crash for a few, then get back up and get back after it. If R&R were not mandatory, you'd see people willingly staying in theater for the entire year, working themselves to exhaustion every night. Eventually, they would break.

While the seriousness of the situation is not the same for me as a writer, I'm feeling the effects right now of not wanting to write. Not even not wanting to. Can't. Have tried. I'm completely and utterly sucked dry right now. I've got three books half written, well over the 60K mark. I'm trying to edit a fourth. And I have nothing left to pull from. I haven't really written in days now. Days. The only time this year that I haven't written was when I was on R&R or otherwise completely overcome by the day job.

Right now, I've got nothing. I'm wrung out.

I have to refill my well. I don't know how much time it will take for that to happen. I don't know how long the funk will last. But I'm reading. I'm thinking about the projects I need to finish so that they're at least ready for when my agent asks for them. But I'm not writing. I'm exercising. Part of the problem is that I've been either sick or hurt for the last three weeks. It's very frustrating for me. I spent half a week on pain meds and actually ended up laid up in bed (trust me: that never happens, until it does). I still wrote then.

But now, I'm simply exercising and reading. I'm lifting weights and doing cardio. I'm not taking breaks from working out because I've been on a break and my body and my mind were suffering for it. I'm reading everything. I'm reading Roxanne St. Claire because she's a master at sexual tension and suspense. I'm reading Allison Brennan because I love her style. I'm reading Laura Kinsale because her emotional hits are the best out there. I'm reading Sherry Thomas and Laura Griffin. I'm going through about a book a day because all I'm doing is reading. I'm taking notes and marking pages where I can learn.

But mostly, I'm simply reading for enjoyment. Since 2007, I've written almost every day. When it was hard, my writing goal was 1000 words a day. Now, I shoot for 2000 because I know I can do it and because I have to do it. Since 2007, I've written six books, and that does not include complete rewrites of three or the three that I've started and put on the back burner.

All while being unpublished. I wrote and rewrote and crammed as much learning as I possibly could into every minute I had to myself because I want to be published. I want to write for a living. I want this and I want this badly so that in eight years or so, I can join the ranks of the full-time writers.

It's worth the sacrifice but I've learned a valuable lesson. I need to take breaks.

Sometimes, I need to curl up on the couch and just watch a movie. Sometimes, I need to get a good night's sleep and go for a walk without trying to figure out my next plot points.

Sometimes, I just need to refill the well before it runs completely dry.

Monday Music Musings
September 28, 2009

LAST WEEK, ROXANNE ST. Claire had a fantastic post over on Murder She Writes about her muse, or lack thereof. Her position is that the muse isn't real, but a kick-in-the-pants friend to lean on is what most authors depend on.

I agree. Mostly.

I have a muse. It's not something that's separate from me or a being all its own that shimmers around my brain and tells me what to write. But I most definitely have a muse. Mine has been decidedly cranky lately. Last week, I posted about needing to refill my well. My inspiration seemed to have run out on my military romances for a minute. I honest-to-God tried all of my tricks for getting back into my story after the revisions for my agent. I was stuck. I simply ran out of I-give-a-damn for that particular book (not the one I sent to my agent, the other one).

When it got right down to it, I'd pulled a whole lot of military angst out of my well over the last few months. I rewrote After the War, completely, from scratch. I rewrote Burning Out, completely, from scratch. Both projects were easily enough rewritten because I opted to keep nothing from the previous incarnations except the characters and even most of those were gone or revamped. I started writing Derrick's story. That was dark and deep, and I know exactly where it's going but I just can't seem to get into his head right now.

I feel guilty on those days I'm not writing but I really had nothing to give. So, you know what?

I put them away. I set aside the military stuff for a time. I figured my agent has a solid copy now on the first book and my CP has the second book. Book three can go on the shelf for a little while until I get refilled. In the meantime, my paranormal has been talking to me.

Actually, it's been whispering to me out of the darkness, which makes for a seriously creepy walk to the showers at midnight in the pitch black that is the Mosul night. But it's been occupying my thoughts and so I started rereading. Opened the Word document so that I can comment like I was CPing someone else's work. And yeah, it needs a ton of work. But the cool part is that I've brainstormed what happens in the next two books, which makes the first book easier to reform into something somewhat coherent.

The very best part, though, that made my muse incredibly happy was finding new music. It's dark and deep and exactly what I need to be listening to in order to write this paranormal.

My muse is not a separate thing but it is tied into certain habits and the one habit guaranteed to make me and my muse deliriously happy enough to crank out serious revisions is good tunes. Tunes that I can't get out of my head are the perfect thing for me to write to. I don't know why but there is a direct correlation to my having music stuck in my head and my level of productivity. NOT creativity, because that comes with the productivity. But when I get something stuck in my head, it's a good sign that I've got some serious word counts coming.

Thank you, Signs of Betrayal, for a rocking good album and for kick-starting my muse!

The Silence of the Pen (As It Were)
September 30, 3009

LAST WEEK WAS A good one, though you'd never know it by the sound of the crickets coming from my blog. Somehow, I managed to dig back into the writing scene, having cranked out a good 50+ pages on my paranormal while I wait on comments from my agent on another book. The paranormal is a little different for me, in that I really struggled at first to get into my heroine's head. I ended up starting over and finding a way in and it feels so good to be writing again.

I was really concerned over the last few weeks. I literally stared at my MacBook and nothing came. I couldn't summon the concern for my characters to even reread from the beginning to pick up whatever it was that I'd lost. That technique failed me. So I took a break, thinking that a day or so wouldn't hurt.

Surprise. That break turned into three weeks. I was definitely in a depression, though I couldn't see my way out at the time. I started back on my vitamins and got into a good argument and magically, I felt like writing again. It's sad but my no arguing pledge to my commander apparently sucked the life out of my muse as well. It seems I have a small problem with conflict in my life, in that I really do thrive on it.

That is not a good thing but at this point, I'm not going to argue with whatever gets my butt in a chair and words coming out of my fingertips once more.

At this point, I'm just excited to be writing again and enjoying it.

Preparing for Redeployment
October 1, 2009

I JUST CAME FROM a redeployment briefing. One of the many things the Army excels at is killing you slowly with briefings. I had to listen to six different people talk about how not to kill yourself and how to balance your checkbook upon returning home. Our chaplain actually gave a really great presentation about reintegrating with your spouse when you get home and to take things slowly.

But nothing there really meant anything to me. The battlemind training doesn't apply to FOBbits. I've never left the wire, nothing has blown up next to me. All in all, I've just worked seven days a week for the last year and occasionally kitted up to visit an outsite.

I've got no reason to be anxious about going home.

Except that I am. And I think I do.

See, most folks are going home to the barracks or to a spouse. They have a place to go to. I'm going to a house that will have been devoid of human and animal life (at least I hope animal life, otherwise, it's going to be a sad-faced day explaining why I'm screaming at the huge spider in my foyer, but that's another story and another house). I've got to wait somewhere around three weeks before I can leave and go round up the family and by family, I mean children, cats, and dogs (thank God I've convinced my five year old that her bunny's life span will be significantly longer if they stay at Grammy's house).

The list of what I have to do in that three-week period feels a little overwhelming. I'm not looking forward to shopping for a new washer and dryer. I don't want to go grocery shopping. I don't want to have to rush home from work every night, sit in traffic, and cook dinner only to have my five year old refuse to eat (to everyone who said she'd grow out of it, she didn't, it's worse now). I don't want to go to Starbucks and I don't want to sit on a flight in Killeen waiting to take off for Bangor.

All in all, life is simpler over here and when I think about everything that I have to resume doing when I get home, I get a little anxious. I've discovered I dislike busses, which I assume is going to transfer to a really fun flight. I get nervous in intersections. I haven't petted a dog in months and I haven't had a psychotic cat licking my pillow near my head all year long.

There's so much that goes into daily life at home and that doesn't include the fact that I'm hoping to be a real writer at some point and actually sell a book or three. That's just more time that I really don't think I have. I can't stay up all night writing because I have to be up at 5 for PT.

It's a little disconcerting to be feeling anxious about going home when I should be happy and looking forward to it.

Truth be told, I'm pretty damn anxious.

Anger Management: Real Life and Fiction
October 9, 2009

WHAT REALLY MAKES YOU mad? I mean, gets your blood pressure up to where you could really start screaming at someone. Or are you the kind of person who gets really quiet when things start to piss you off?

Me? I'm a screamer. I'm already a loud person but when I really get going, everyone knows and gives me a wide berth. That's not necessarily a good thing. I've mellowed significantly as I've aged but certain things still set me off.

When my sense of right and wrong is violated, I get really angry. I've worked hard on getting over the fact that some people in my section still have jobs. While I'm responsible up to a point for at least one of those people, the fact that higher up made bad decisions really chaps my sense of right and wrong, especially during war.

But what about your characters? I see characters who flip out over the slightest miscommunication, turning into the Big Mis (big misunderstanding for you non-romance readers). But if something can be solved with a simple conversation, is it really a Big Mis or contrived for the plot?

Here's the thing and I've mentioned it before: communication is not easy. It's not like everyone wakes up in the morning and says, "I think I'll bare my soul to this person today." It's incredibly hard for me to admit in real life to my husband that the thought of going back and being a full-time mom, soldier, author, housekeeper is a little unnerving. So why do we have expectations for our characters to sit down and talk about it when it's one of the hardest things for us to do? Our heroines especially get blasted for not telling all, such as revealing a deeply held insecurity that is the cause of friction in the fictional relationship.

And that's just simple communication. What about those hot button issues (in my case certain folks still having jobs) that send your character to climbing the walls? If you haven't set it up correctly, when your character does lose his or her mind, it might seem overblown. But a careful balance is required in that you don't repeat yourself (a problem I have both in real life and in fiction).

So how do you create characters who are passionate about things? How do you keep your heroines from looking like shrill harpies and your heroes from looking like they're overreacting? What elements do you weave in to avoid the big reveal but to have the reader pull back the layers like an onion, slowly and carefully so that they really care about what makes your character tick?

Something Neat From a Year in Iraq
October 13, 2009

AS MUCH AS THERE have been some significant challenges this year, there have also been a couple of really cool things. I've gone on my first Black Hawk flight. I've experienced my first earthquake.

I've also gotten something that most married folks don't get until the kids leave for college. I got my husband back.

Now, I'm not saying that it was like a reunion or anything but when there are kids around, you're Mommy and Daddy, not husband and wife. Seldom do we get time to just be us. We've had a whole year and you know what's kind of cool? We still really like each other. A lot. We laugh about different things than we did when we were younger, but this is the first real time we've had together—alone—in almost five years, since our oldest daughter was born.

And it's not like we're spending all day, every day together. We have a few minutes at lunch and dinner and maybe an hour or two before we go to bed. It's more than most couples have and less than others, but it works for us. I've learned a lot about him this year, both as a husband and as a soldier. I think he's learned a lot about me and how we've both changed over the last half decade. But the best thing is discovering that there's still a whole lot of love, mixed in with a lot of like, and it's not just the kids holding us together. A lot of couples don't get that, and find themselves wondering what life will be like without the glue of the kids making them stick.

He's seen me through some tough times this year. When the swine flu panic hit and I was a walking panic attack, he and I planned our escape route should the world go to shit and we need to get home (he was only half joking). He made me laugh when all I wanted to do was cry for missing the kids. And we laughed about the torment our kids put my mom through, knowing we were both going to be frustrated with them within two weeks of getting home.

It's been an unstated assumption in the Army, since the war started, that deployments can make good marriages stronger but destroy weak ones. This is my husband's third and my first. I look to him as the voice of experience and he's talked me through some of my fears. I'm glad I've gotten this time with my husband the man, not the daddy.

So getting to be husband's wife this year, even with everything else that's gone on, is at least one good thing that's come out of being in Iraq.

The Writing on the (Latrine) Wall
October 14, 2009

I'M GOING TO TAKE something funny from Iraq and turn it into a life lesson for writers (myself included). There is a point to this, I swear.

I made the latrine wall.

There's no doubt it was me because, heh, they used my name. They said I was a reject. Okay, so not really a painful jab like "LT is a dirty slut" or something more creative, but it was there in black and bad penmanship for everyone to read. "LT is a reject."

I'm leaving it up.

It's going to make me a better author.

No, this isn't going to teach me to write like Poe or any of the greats.

It's about the heat that's going to come when I become a published author. I write about soldiers. I write about Iraq and the things that soldiers have done. I'm not pulling my punches. I can wish all day long that I wasn't a blunt person but at the end of the day, I'm writing what speaks to me about the experiences I've gone through and other soldiers have gone through.

I know that not everyone is going to like what I've written. I know that there will be people who know me who think I'll have gotten things wrong or something else that they will take viscerally to heart. And there will be negative blog comments and negative personal attacks.

I'm sure of it. I'll have fellow officers question me and my ability to be a writer and an officer. I'll have others call me a tramp for writing about sex.

The dislike and the virulence is going to be there. That doesn't mean I'm going to stop writing the books that speak to me, just like I'm not going to stop being the officer and the leader that I am. I make mistakes. You've read about a lot of them here because I hope people can at least learn from the mistakes that I've made along the way, as an officer, a soldier, a working mom, and as a writer.

I'm not perfect. I have a hard time telling people the truth but when it needs to be done, I do it in person, not in some passive aggressive way like writing it on the latrine wall. In my opinion, that's like posting a vicious attack online and doing it anonymously.

So I'm leaving the reject comment up, just like I'm going to try and deal with negative online comments and negative backlash. You can't help what people think. You can only do the best you can, learn from your mistakes and try to grow as a person in whatever role you're in.

Writing: Work or Not?
October 19, 2009

THIS WEEKEND'S #WRITECHAT ON Twitter asked a question: is writing working or not and did it matter? To both questions I say: yes, it is work and yes, it matters that you think of it that way. Here's why.

If you're working, you're getting paid for something or you have a reasonable assumption of getting paid down the road for the fruits of your labor. Just because you're not out slinging a pick ax doesn't mean you're not working. Additionally, if you are going to try and get published, then writing is your job or it will be in the future. Just because you don't have to leave the house in order to do it, doesn't mean it gets pushed to the side. If you honestly want to be published, then long hours of practice and work are required.

I never in a million years thought that writing a book was going to be hard. And you know what? It wasn't hard to write that first one. The multiple rewrites, the revisions and the edits? That was work and hard. You write words down, you build this scene, and then with the stroke of a few keys, it's gone, no matter how much you love it, because it doesn't advance the story.

But is it work? I say yes, writing is work.

But on the flip side of that argument, it doesn't feel like work because I love it. I read a quote somewhere that if you love what you do, you'll never work a day in your life, and I think that's correct. I can sit at my computer for hours, working through a scene, finding the right words or ruthlessly culling my darlings, and it never feels like work.

On that note, I need limits.

Because it doesn't feel like work, I can and do let it take up most of my free time, especially over here in Iraq where there aren't competing priorities, like laundry. I feel like if I'm not writing, I'm slacking off, but that's simply not the case. I need time to recharge. If I'm always working on a book, I'm not reading a book, or I'm not taking a break for me. Reading is fundamental to being a writer and if I'm trying to be any good, I need to read books that challenge me, which takes time.

Thinking of writing as a job means that I need to work on it for a time, then set it aside. It doesn't matter if I don't feel like I need a break, at the end of the day I do. So I set #writegoals for the day and try to stick to them. That way, once they're met, I can step away while still feeling like I've accomplished enough for the day. Plus, just because I haven't sat down with my manuscript doesn't mean I haven't worked. I spent the weekend editing my latest project. That was work. When it was done and mailed to my agent, I took a break, sinking into a novel rather than opening up Scrivener.

If you want to be a professional writer, don't quit but don't overdo it. There's a time and a place for all things and that includes writing. I can't not write, but I also have other responsibilities, like living, being my husband's wife and my children's mom. So don't let writing take over your life, no matter how much you enjoy it.

Treat it like a job, albeit a job you enjoy.

Synchronicity or Plagiarism?
October 19, 2009

DO YOU EVER GET that "oh shit" feeling when you read something that sounds an awful lot like something you've written?

That just happened and I can't help feeling like I'm going to be accused of being a hack. I've got a sick feeling in my stomach and I can't figure out why, because I've done nothing wrong.

Back in August, I started the fifth book in my War's Darkest series. I got about halfway through and set it aside because another work needed my attention. In my book, my character Derrick Rierson sees a little girl everywhere he looks. I haven't yet worked out what happened to him or what he did to make him see her but I know the little girl is a key piece of his damnation and his ultimate salvation.

I just opened the first page of David Finkel's The Good Soldiers and read about a soldier who sees a little girl when he closes his eyes.

Does it matter that I wrote my story before I ever even heard of The Good Soldiers? I don't know. Does it matter that JoAnn Ross and I both wrote a book titled Shattered with a lead character named Shane? I don't know. But as the yet unpublished author, I now know what it feels like to be worried about being accused of plagiarism.

I pulled the idea of the little girl out of the ether but it turns out, it wasn't from a void. It really happened to a soldier and now I've got to decide whether or not to keep my book the way it is or change it.

I won't make any decisions right now. I'll finish writing my book and I'll still read Mr. Finkel's book. I'll discuss with my agent and the writers in my circle of trust. But I do know that I'm considering making a change because of the possibility of accusation, not an actual accusation.

So writers: do you change your books because someone else has the same idea or do you stubbornly hold onto the idea that sparked the initial work?

Reliable Old Friends: Revisiting Your Favorite Books
October 20, 2009

I'M LYING IN MY CHU, sick again from the unending parade of bugs that have decided to take root in my digestive system this year. I swear, American stomach flu and common cold have nothing on the Iraqi versions. I feel like I've been sick every other week this entire year. But I'll get better and move on, just like always.

But I'm lying here, and I'm staring at a copy of Anne McCaffrey's Dragonflight. I've been dying to get home to my collection of Anne's books and reread the series. It's been a favorite of mine since I discovered Moreta's Ride and was utterly and completely confused as to what it meant for a dragon queen to clutch. Then I discovered Dragonflight and my confusion was answered with a burning need to read everything that Ms. McCaffrey ever wrote about Pern. Unfortunately, the second book in her series, Dragonquest, was misplaced on the library shelves and I refused to read on until I could read the series in sequence. This was before I had a car and before the days of Amazon when I could simply order the next book. I still remember my joy—yes joy—when I found it on the shelf in the wrong place, with the As instead of the Ms and was able to read the next story.

I'm looking at the cover of the book and remembering all those fond hours as a child disappearing into the world of Pern and wishing beyond wish that I could have a dragon. Cut me some slack, I was a lonely kid.

But now, it's been years since I reread the story and I certainly haven't reread it since I became a writer. The last book in the series I loved was the Masterharper of Pern. So it's been a while since I traveled there and lost myself in the world. I'm looking at the cover and wondering, will the lore still pull me in? Will the book still speak to me as it did throughout my middle grade years and into adulthood? Or will my writer's eye see things that I never noticed before, ruining the world I've loved for as long as I can remember?

I felt the same trepidation when I decided to reread Laura Kinsale's books. I loved her books as a young woman but was nervous that they might not hold the same thrall they had when I was younger. I worried that my ability to get lost in the story might have been lost to me as I started looking at the words instead of at the story.

It's the mark of a great writer to be able to pull a writer into the story and not let them go. I read Laura Kinsale's Seize the Fire this year for the first time and the story pulled me in so hard, I skipped out of work to finish it. I cared so deeply for the characters, I wept at the end. That is the mark of a great writer. Not just words on pages, but words that create a story and pull the reader into the world.

I've cracked open the first page of Anne McCaffrey's Dragonflight and was immediately seized by the opening sentence. "Lessa woke, cold." Her world immediately pulled me back in, dragging me across the skies to my favorite haunt as a child. It's the goal we should all strive for as authors, to create a world, whatever world we chose to write in, and pull our readers in. We have to make them care about the characters.

Editor extraordinaire Kate Duffy told me once that my characters were too real, that they weren't doing anything better than a real person might and readers read to escape. I did a lot of soul searching after she was good enough to take the time to make those comments to me, over the phone. She impacted me because she told me the characters felt real, just not better than us.

How do you pull your reader into your world? How do you make them care about the characters so much that they have to turn the page and see what happens next?

When you figure that out, let me know.

Empowering Women: Romance's Subversion
October 22, 2009

I'VE STARTED THIS BLOG post four different times today but I think I finally found a way into it. I've been doing a lot of thinking this week about women in the military as well as women in romance.

A recent Newsweek article about female genital mutilation struck me forcibly. In the article, a woman named Sila, who chose to have reconstructive surgery to repair her clitoris—which was removed by other women in her clan—said that she enjoys romance novels because she wishes she could have "that". Karin Tabke, a romance author whose book Sila mentions she read, points out that her romance novel is referred to as a "little joke". In her response to the article Karin Tabke says that she's tired of romance being jilted. She argues that romance is empowering.

I've kind of stayed out of the argument as to whether romance is empowering or not until now.

I've been a student of religion for a long time and while my own religious tradition is Catholic, I challenge the idea that still holds in the Church that I am resigned to two roles: either whore or mother (Magdalene or Mary). I'm hoping to set a different role model for my daughters outside those constraints.

What does this have to do with romance? Well, in the traditional religions, women are subjected to their husband's wills. It is glaringly obvious in certain parts of the world that being an unattached woman means being vulnerable. Witness Africa, where rape is a tool of war and even being married is not a guarantee of safety. Women in this part of the world are limited in their world view in that they only have their mothers to look to as role models and their mothers are concerned with the more immediate problems of survival rather than women's liberation. And female genital mutilation is performed and approved of by the women in their culture, all to gain acceptance by the male dominated society. This isn't the point of this post, merely I'm using it to point out that men have taken away women's power and convinced them that it is a good thing.

When Sila in the Newsweek article states that "she wishes she could be like" the women she reads about in romance novels, I was moved, deeply. Romance novels are empowering for women. It gives us as women strong heroines to look to who are navigating what is still strongly a man's world, regardless of their chosen profession. By giving a woman like Sila permission to crave her own sexuality—that is pleasure in herself as a woman, not as a thing for men to enjoy only—romance has brought awareness to another generation of women that we are not the root of all evil in the world, which is still a majority opinion in many of the traditional religions that blanket the world.

Romance is derided because women write it, among other reasons. I think it's derided because it's subversive. What could be worse than taking sexual power away from the head of the nuclear family—the man—and giving it to women? Not only are we taking power from a man, but we are claiming it for ourselves and that includes sexual pleasure.

This is not without consequences. Violence against women is rising around the world, both as a tool of war and as a reflection of a loss of power. While I'm not going into the discussion of rape here, I will say that as a soldier, the question of how I appear to my male counterparts is a direct reflection of me as a woman, not just as a soldier. No matter how much I might want to be one of the guys, I'm not. I'm also in a unique position over here because I go to chow and the gym with my husband: ergo, I don't get a lot of sexual male attention. This is okay with me, but I tend to have a very visceral response to male attention. I don't want it. I want to do my job. I don't want special favors as a woman. But I won't go to the chow hall without my husband because I can feel the eyes and the stares and I feel dirty because of it. Other women here have to deal with that daily. Some welcome it, others don't, but it is the cost of doing business as a woman in the military.

But what about those women who are over here that do want to be women first, soldiers second? What about those women who like the male attention or who wear makeup simply because it makes them feel good? What about those women who have no idea how to be one of the guys because the notion is as foreign to them as being a flirty girly-girl to me is? Are they wrong? Am I?

I don't know. I think it requires balance and if you choose to highlight yourself as a woman, you will necessarily lose credibility among the males around you. I see it right now, when two girly-girls moved into the TOC. They are the subject of ridicule because they spend more time on their hair than their reports. Has anyone ever told them that to their face?

Because here's another dirty little secret: we're our own biggest cheerleaders and toughest critics. A female editor is more likely to hammer a manuscript if she thinks it's been written by a woman. A female officer is more likely to be harder on her female lieutenants than a male officer is.

I think having a dialogue about empowering women—both in the military and in the writing world—involves many factors. I know kickass field-grade officers who read Christina Dodd. I know I've passed along Sherry Thomas and Laura Kinsale, among others, to the female sergeants I work with. I've had discussions about romance with male soldiers—who have never read a romance novel but deride it nonetheless. The role of women in our society can be tied to the perceptions of romance as a genre.

I think we need to start by mentoring and raising our daughters to look beyond Bratz dolls and princesses. There is a female major who takes young women aside and teaches and mentors them that there is more to life than getting a male's attention. Over here in Iraq, it's too easy to fall into the "queen for a year" mentality and reduce our effectiveness so that it becomes solely based on what can we get because someone wants to sleep with us.

So we need to mentor. The RWA is a fantastic example of mentorship in action. Experienced women writers team up with newbies and provide mentorship and training in the writing world. In the military world, however, we tend to ostracize those who don't fit into our mold of what right looks like.

As the romance genre continues to evolve and the discussion of women's roles in the military continue to evolve because the battlefield will remain nonlinear for the next few wars, we as women will have to continue to look at our roles in society and our contribution to it.

Are we simply whores or mothers or are we something else entirely, starting with individuals? I'd argue that romance provides an example, in all its raw claiming of sexuality and the pleasure that we are now allowed to have in it, that can serve as a role model. There are some craptastically terrible books out there, just as there are female soldiers who are happy to screw their way to a good report card, but there are also books that challenge the very meaning of what happiness means and defines new roles for women. And there are female soldiers who earn the respect of their peers by being a bad-ass fifty cal gunner.

We are more than mother or whore and the romance genre leads the way in showing us possibilities beyond both stereotypes.

Continue the subversion, ladies. We've got daughters looking up to us.

Memorial
October 23, 2009

I DON'T THINK ANYONE enjoys memorial ceremonies, but they are a poignant reminder of what we risk when we deploy. Regardless of political or religious beliefs, at the end of the day, we are all soldiers and we all have a job to do that helps the soldier to your left and right make it home.

I never could hear Taps as a kid without tearing up. Now, it is impossible. The American flag carries a different symbolism for me. The men and women who join our Army in a time of war are joining knowing they are deploying to combat. They leave fathers and mothers, sons and daughters, husbands and wives back in the rear while they go and live and fight and die in a far off country.

I can't explain the pull, the need to be with your soldiers. I can't explain why a man would cut a cast from his arm in order to go and fight to find his buddies pinned down in a city.

But just because I can't explain it, doesn't make it any less real. And the pain of losing a soldier is something that changes the men and women that soldier fought and lived with. We remember the good, we laugh about the fun times but in the end, we pay tribute to a young soldier who died doing what they wanted to be doing.

We all volunteered to be here. Maybe not in Iraq, but we volunteered to serve.

Take a moment today to remember all those who have gone before us. The soldiers who gave their lives in the many wars in our Nation's history. Their names are different but they all died a hero's death and you don't have to know a soldier to feel the pain of their loss.

To our fallen, thank you for making the ultimate sacrifice. Our prayers are with your families.

Another Missed Birthday
October 25, 2009

TODAY IS MY YOUNGEST daughter's third birthday. We were lucky enough to have been there for the ones prior to this. We missed our oldest daughter's third, fourth, and fifth.

I decided yesterday to watch movies. Old movies of when our youngest was a baby and our oldest was a rambunctious two year old. But what really got me was the video I had of three days after youngest was born. My oldest and my husband sat on the couch, holding her. My oldest had a look of wonder in her eyes as she looked up at her Daddy. She just wanted to "hol' her."

It was such a wild time for her. When we came home on mid-tour, she had the same look on her face. Awe. Disbelief. A stunned smile as if she couldn't quite believe that we were both there on my mom's porch.

My youngest is a little different. We might have made it to her birthdays, but we've both missed more than half her life. My mom will have done all the potty training. She saw her walk. She's been the one to hold her when she's gotten sick and run her to the doctors to find out why she stopped talking after we left again.

So whereas our oldest ran out to greet us, our youngest was a few steps behind. She hid around the sliding glass door and for a moment, she wouldn't come out. Then, she shrieked "Mommy!" and ran toward me (she wasn't a big fan of her Daddy for quite a while).

I've given up more than half my youngest daughter's life. My dad drove me to the airport when she was barely seven months old for me to go to officer training. I didn't see her again until she was almost a year. And she'd forgotten me when I did finally graduate from OCS.

So when I say that time is the one thing you can't get back, I'm not exaggerating. I'm not just missing pictures of birthdays. I'm missing whole years of their lives.

We're down to less than 45 days before we get back to the States. I know it'll be insane, trying to adjust from being just a soldier to being all those things that a mom is simply by virtue of being a mom. I know I'll be busy then, because life is simpler over here in Iraq, but I'll give up the simplicity just to be able to feel my daughters' arms around my neck and know they're safe and sound and tucked into bed a few feet away.

Happy Birthday, baby girl. We'll see you soon.

Saying Thank You
October 25, 2009

THIS WEEK, SKYLER WHITE, author of the upcoming January release of And Falling, Fly posted on her blog about how grateful she was to Julie Kenner and Anya Bast for taking the time to give her quotes for her book. It was a reminder to me of just how generous the writing community is as a whole, but romance writers specifically.

As this year in Iraq winds down, I realize that I have a whole lot to be grateful for. It's been a long year with some rough patches but it was made easier for me by a whole lot of people.

I've been meaning to post this for a while but Skye has motivated me to get off my butt, especially considering that I'll be losing internet service shortly and will fall off the planet for a few weeks until we get home.

I'm going to miss people because I've tried to keep track and failed. This year has been a rough one in many ways but I'm grateful for everyone's support. If I don't mention you, it's not for lack of gratitude, it's because I'm an airhead.

Thank you to everyone in the RWA who answered the call for school supplies for Iraqi kids.

Thank you to everyone who sent their books over here for soldiers to read.

Thank you to every author who trucked a copy of their book to the post office, so I could share the new release. I passed along every copy, to get the word out of your fantastic books.

Thank you, Lexi Connor, for standing in line for me at RWA National and getting books signed, then trucking them to the post office and sending me cards from your class.

Thank you, Jane Perrine for emailing me once a week and just saying hi.

Thank you, Candace Irvin, for kicking me in the ass when I wanted to quit.

Thank you, Darcy Saint Amant, for letting me lean on you for officer advice.

Thank you, CSM Bill Crain, for kicking me in the ass when I made stupid lieutenant mistakes and for supporting me through some rough LT moments.

Thank you, Al Harris, for house sitting and making me laugh. I hope you and my mom didn't talk about anything too embarrassing.

Thank you, Michelle McGinnis, for unscrewing my blog when I crashed it. What took me 48 hours to screw up, you fixed in 20 minutes.

Thank you, Isabel from SFWA and your critique partners, who mailed my Gotcha contest final in for me to the publisher.

Thank you, JoAnn Ross, for giving me a quote for War's Darkest Fear and for sharing a character named Shane.

Thank you, Laura Kinsale, for being sweet enough to answer a random tweet and send me an ARC of Lessons in French. That tweet was just the beginning.

Thank you, Roxanne St. Claire, for sending me your Bullet Catchers Series and a ton of chocolate and for letting me pick your brain on what could make my writing better.

Thank you to everyone who friended me on Facebook (I just joined this year) and for following me on Twitter.

Thank you for those of you who posted on my blog even when your comments disagreed with mine. I love a good discussion and I'm glad to have been part of the debate over whatever we talked about this year.

Thank you, RomVets, for answering the call in so many ways. You ladies paved the way for me to be here now and for that, thanks is not enough.

Thank you, Austin RWA. You gals (and Gary) supported me in a way that brings tears to my eyes just thinking about it. From sending me books to the emails that just said hi, this year was so much less lonely because I had you. Your friendship means so much to me, more than you'll ever know.

Thank you, SB Sarah, for using me in a blog post on your site and for introducing me to the world of Smart Bitches and a whole lot of good laughs along the way.

Thank you, Evelyn Palfrey, for adopting my soldiers and making sure all of my girls and my friend Tamara in Afghanistan had the right stuff for their hair.

Thank you, Cindy Gerard, for the emails and school supplies. You rounded up so much support for the kids.

Thank you, Sarah, Tigris Eden, and Colleen Thompson, for the mentions and the guest blogging opportunities.

Thank you, Teresa Bodwell, for your amazing insight and for letting me be a part of Unleash Your Story. It was an honor to be able to blog for an awesome cause.

Thank you, Julie Kenner, for tearing through my manuscript and helping me get it ready for my agent and for so much more that only you and I will ever know.

Thank you, Kim Whalen, for taking me on when I was half a world away and despite the fact that I need lots of TLC.

To my husband, who still loves me after spending a year in a 12' x 8' room and putting up with my can't-put-stuff-away-itis.

But to my mom, who raised my babies this year, who harassed the living crap out of me when I asked about a fever. You went from Grammy to Mom overnight. My girls are better for having spent this year and most of 2007 with you. I can't wait to get them home, but know this: I could not have done this year without you. Thank you, for loving my babies better than your own.

I know I'm forgetting people and for that I'm sorry. There will probably be a Part Two, just because I'm going to forget and need to add more. Just know that I am incredibly grateful for all the support and all of our soldiers are grateful for every care package and every email.

Growing
October 26, 2009

I'M NOT TALKING ABOUT my ass, either. This year has been an experience for me, in so many ways, it's hard to count. But you know me, I'm going to try anyway.

As a soldier, I've grown because I understand the need for pragmatism. When I was a private or a sergeant looking up at the seniors in my company, I never understood some decisions that were made. Now, I think I can at least look at a decision and understand why, even if I still disagree with the what. That doesn't mean I'm going to let it go, if it's something I feel very strongly about, but I at least try to understand where someone else is coming from.

Taking that angle in trying to understand decisions from higher, I look for motivations to try and make my characters stronger, better and more realistic. I look at hard decisions that have been made over here and I put them on paper. I'm absolutely sure that my interpretation is different from what the folks experienced on the ground, but I'm trying to understand. I think in a very real way, writing about being over here has helped me channel some of the fear that I hold inside me that today might be the day the shit hits the fan. Am I ready?

As a soldier, I've tried—and failed—to maintain relationships. I'm very much a believer in saying what you mean and I have an incredibly hard time dealing with people who say one thing to my face and do something else behind my back. I generally try not to deal with them, but once more, I try to understand. When it comes to posting on my blog, everything has been tempered with asking myself "What if my brigade commander reads this?" or "What would my friends Darcy (as an officer and as a friend) or Bill (as a CSM and a friend) say?" I've tried to maintain professionalism both publicly and privately and still struggle with this. There have been errors in judgment on my part and I won't try to excuse them, just know that I've learned from them.

I learned some powerful lessons about loyalty this year, both as a writer and as a soldier. When you have loyalty to someone, you expect that it is returned. It might not be and when that happens, it's a major shift in how the world upholds balance. When loyalty is betrayed in a public sense, it's all the more difficult to deal with. I have loyalty in odd places and, in other instances, they make perfect sense. I have incredible loyalty to soldiers on the ground who are accused because no one knows what decisions they've had to make or how they made them. I won't defend some decisions because they are anathema to everything we stand for as soldiers but I won't say I won't try to understand. I do know that a soldier on the ground makes a thousand life-altering decisions in the space of seconds, so I try to understand that before I step aside and let the stone throwing begin.

As a writer, my single biggest accomplishment (other than landing a fab agent) was learning to revise my own stuff. Working with an awesome critique partner taught me how to look at her stuff and say why something was bothering me. In turn, I was able to take that same skill and start applying it to my writing. I've still got miles to go before this skill gets to where it needs to be, but I've at least been able to look at that and say nah, you need to go, the whole thing, and I'm starting over. So we'll see what happens when I start revising that second book.

This year in Iraq has not been easy. I've struggled with depression and insomnia. I haven't used my insomnia to write—but I'm fixing to. If I can't sleep, I might as well get out of bed and do something worthwhile. I've read and read and read some more and learned so much about writing and different authors and techniques. I've added some new favorites to my list of Will Read Everything They Write and I'm always open to suggestions for something new. I learned a lot about the publishing industry as a whole, just as I've learned about how the Army works and the ever present pragmatism, regardless of the ideals you might hope for.

The whole point of this post is to keep learning and keep watching. There are character studies all around you. Look at a reaction and try to figure out where they're coming from. Never pass up a moment to learn from something or someone around you. I've had some great teachers and I'm just grateful they haven't given up on me, because I've learned some powerful lessons this year.

The Impostor Within
October 28, 2009

I READ A BLOG somewhere in the last few weeks that talked about feeling like an impostor. Like everything you'd done was a sham and that someone was going to come along and expose you.

That's me. I've been in the Army for fourteen years and despite everything I've done, I feel like I've been faking it. I know that's not a good description but it's the best I can come up with. I feel like I haven't worked hard enough, that this deployment hasn't really been that tough, that my books are never going to be good enough.

I'm my own worst critic. I've heard a lot of authors talk about self doubt but mine is a never-ending struggle to overcome that little voice inside that says "you're a sham." If I've won a contest, it must have been that mine was the least bad of the entries. If I've had stuff requested, it was on a promise in the query that did not materialize in the manuscript. I feel like everything I've done, I could do better. I have an unending drive to make my book better, to the point that I must stop because I might be screwing it up rather than making it better. I'll work on a manuscript until the words blur and I've memorized the pattern, but that doesn't mean I'm actually succeeding in making it better.

So what brought this on? We had an awards ceremony today where members of the brigade staff and my battalion were awarded Bronze Stars. While I could easily look across the six rows of officers and NCOs and see those that worked their asses off, I felt a hot distaste as I looked and saw those who'd done nothing to deserve a Bronze Star as a "Thanks for Playing" award. Lest you get confused, I don't feel like I deserved one, either. There are soldiers in my company who deserve this award more than I do.

I look at the comment that still sits like a black slash alone on the latrine wall and wonder if the person who wrote it sees something that others either don't see or won't say. I feel like in everything

I do, it's not good enough or that it wasn't really that hard.

I look back on my year in Iraq and I have done nothing to deserve this award. I look at all the awards on my chest and many of them are awards for winning boards. It's hard for me to accept that I've earned them or to hear that I have a reputation for working hard, because I don't feel like it's all that hard.

I've learned some difficult lessons this year, the hardest being that you can't change the system. I don't know when I made the change from idealist to cynical pragmatist, but it happened. Maybe it was before I became an officer, maybe it was after, but the system is too big for me to change.

But at the end of it all, I don't deserve the recognition I received and I feel like sooner or later, someone is going to see that and call my bluff.

Thank You Part 2
October 28, 2009

I TOLD YOU I was going to forget and these are along the lines of "how could I possibly have forgotten." But I did, so there you go.

I'm correcting my egregious oversights now. But rest assured, there will probably be more.

Thank you, Irene Preston, for trucking hundreds of pounds of care packages and books from ARWA to the post office and mailing them to me.

Thank you, Teresa Medeiros, for not banishing me from Twitter when I tweeted a secret (and for the massive care package). :)

Thank you, Emily McKay, who sent my babies Easter bunnies and little monkeys and said they were from me.

Thank you, Wendy Rome, for sending my soldiers Taco Night. It was a huge success and started a trend in my company.

People's generosity this year is simply astonishing and I can't thank you enough for your support!

Falling in Love Again or Trying Something New?
October 29, 2009

SO IT WOULD BE kind of funny if as a writer, I didn't love books. But I really love them. I love the feel of a fresh spine beneath my fingers, the smooth edge of a cover not yet opened. I love the potential of the story and the promise held between those covers. There are small collections of books over here, scattered around the FOB and I'm drawn to them every time, just to see if it was something I'd read or would enjoy reading.

I have a small confession, however.

Brace yourself.

I'm an incredibly picky reader but I'm a romance writer who, when she started writing romance, did not read romance.

Huh?

When I started writing, I knew it was going to be romance. But when I started writing, the only romance I'd read in years was Nora Roberts and Suzanne Brockmann. I didn't have a clue what was out there market-wise. My mentor Candace Irvin told me to get my ass to the bookstore and start looking for romance novels that were something like what I'd written. I didn't find it (though I discovered I love romantic suspense) and I only recently discovered why, when Roxanne St. Claire asked whether War's Darkest Fear was romantic suspense or straight romance. It's straight romance, which means that, when I was pitching it as a military romance, agents were automatically thinking suspense, but I digress.

When I was a teenager, I discovered Danielle Steel, through my grandmother. I remember reading Zoya and Star and going to the library to read everything she'd written. I moved on to Jackie Collins, who my mother quickly banned from our house. At the time, I was pissed but as the mother of two potential teenagers, I can understand why my mom did not want her then-thirteen year old reading something that...explicit. But my love of romance continued. I grew up reading Johanna Lindsey, Laura Kinsale, and Jude Deveraux.

I can't tell you when I stopped reading romance. I honestly have no idea when or why I stopped. But I went from loving all things historical romance to not reading one in years. Then, in 2001, I picked up Nora Roberts' Dance Upon the Air and slowly reentered the romance world. Suzanne Brockmann made me want to write about the soldiers around me. Honestly, when I joined Austin RWA, I had no idea what I was getting myself into. The wonderful women there were talking about all these authors I'd never heard of. I was completely clueless.

Here's another secret. I had not picked up a historical novel in years. I don't remember the last one I read, but I know that Laura Kinsale's were the only ones I had kept in a box of things from high school (yes, my copy of The Shadow and the Star still has Fabio on it). The first historical I read in years was Sherry Thomas's Private Arrangements. I read it out of loyalty to the group of women who took me in and taught me about the world I'd somehow left behind when I joined the Army.

I loved it. And here's what else. I picked up Julia London's Highland Scandal. Loved it. Teresa Medeiros just sent me a care package that included Tessa Dare, Lisa Kleypas, Jillian Hunter, Eloisa James, and Liz Carlyle. I love them. Every book Teresa sent has been incredible, a reminder of something I used to love and am taking true pleasure in rediscovering.

I'm rediscovering that I enjoy historicals as much as I enjoy romantic suspense. Something I had not experienced in years has seen a reawakening within me. I'm discovering new authors I'd never heard of and finding some that are on my permanent To Be

Read list. I will read every book that Sherry Thomas and Julia London write. I will order Tessa Dare's backlist when I get home, just like I'm eagerly awaiting Laura Griffin's Untraceable, Skyler White's And Falling, Fly, and Julie Kenner's Blood Lily series. A wide spectrum of authors and types of books—that's not a bad thing.

Being over here in Iraq, I've rediscovered romance and that's provided me escape from the realities of Iraq. I didn't like first-person point of view books, but then I read Julie Kenner's Demon Hunting Soccer Mom series. Loved it (seriously laughed my ass off).

So try something new. Don't limit yourself by saying, "I don't like paranormals." Try one. Don't refuse to read a historical. Try one. Ask a friend for a recommendation. But try something new and kick yourself out of the habit of familiar reads. You might just find something new or remember when you liked something different and you might just find the inspiration you need to kick your own writing into gear.

Expectations: Real Life and Writing
October 30, 2009

JANE L. FROM DEAR Author and Sarah Frantz were talking yesterday on Twitter about expectations. Jane tweeted that people identified her as Asian as soon as she walked into a room, whereas she identifies more with being white. Sarah commented that Suzanne Brockmann's books were often praised for her portrayal of a gay man's take on the world but disparaged for missing the mark completely on race.

Those comments really hit me hard because you are defined by expectations of what you appear to be. You are judged and dismissed or accepted within the first few moments of meeting someone. The old saying that you never get a second chance to make a first impression is dead on.

So what does this have to do with writing or the Army? Well, you have to put your best foot forward. A female in the Army who cakes on makeup is going to be dismissed by the combat arms soldiers around her, regardless of her proficiency or skill set. Body language experts tell us that a woman who dresses provocatively will be unable to influence the men around her because they'll be seeing her as a trashy woman instead of a woman who means business. While it's hard for a soldier to dress provocatively, it's still possible to draw attention to yourself as a woman and (fair or not) thus detract from your skills as a soldier.

The same thing holds for writers. Agent Sarah Megibow from the Nelson Literary Agency says that the first thing she does when thinking about requesting a manuscript is Google the author. If there are naked photos of you from Spring Break, she's going to think twice about requesting. Your online presence says so much about you as a writer and as a potential client. Once tweeted, you can never take it back, so think clearly before hitting send.

The Army has a saying that when the central promotion boards meet, they're looking for the total soldier. Commanders are known for Googling officers who are applying for positions and yes, that means checking your Facebook page.

Everything out there adds up to the total package and it only takes one thing to turn someone off forever. A lady forever left the Austin RWA meetings because she was offended by the talk I gave about being a soldier in the Army. I really didn't see anything offensive about it, but then again, I'll never know. So you can't be a hundred percent sure what will offend someone and what won't but try to see something from the outside looking in. If you can do that, you'll succeed in creating a professional appearance and manage what people see of you.

Some things you can't change. You can't change what you look like if you're Asian or African-American or even female. People will judge, harshly and unfairly, based on appearance. On the flip side of that, I won't change the fact that I'm a soldier and proud of what my fellow soldiers have done. I guarantee people will be and have been offended by this blog. I can't change that or rather, I won't, because this is who I am.

But I can work my tail off to make sure that every post I publish won't be difficult for me to explain should my brigade commander look at it. I have friends who've mentioned that maybe I should take down a rant and I've listened, because they're on the outside looking in. Even though my public persona is a writer, I'm also an Army officer and there are things I am not allowed to say. I speak for myself, not the Army. I am not going to comment on official policy as established by law or my commander-in-chief. But I can tell you what being in Iraq is like for me. I can tell you what it's like to work for a captain I don't respect. I can tell you my struggles to be a better leader and the second- and third-order effects of failing to make a decision. And I can tell you what it feels like to stand on an airstrip and salute a flag-draped coffin.

All these things, I believe are appropriate for me to share, as an officer and a writer and mom. I won't post pictures of my kids online, because I'm freaked out about child exploitation. But I'll tell you my daughter's eyes were wide and shocked when we walked up onto the porch of my mom's house.

So manage the things you put out in public. People have expectations of you as a writer.

Try to manage those expectations.

Condense Your Life
October 31, 2009

WHEN THE CAV DEPLOYED the first time to Iraq, I remember the discussion about what we were allowed to take with us. Each soldier would share a 36" x 45" trunk (we call them TAT boxes) with another soldier. That was all the personal gear you were allowed to bring to the war. Your two bags were reserved for gear. NBC gear, uniforms, and PTs. If you were carrying a book, it was on your person because space was limited.

As we've gotten into the hang of deploying, soldiers have gotten better at packing more and more stuff. But I'm wondering: could you collapse your entire life down to two boxes, a duffle bag, and a ruck sack? Looking at my entire life for the last year, it fits into those boxes. And half of one box is all my historical documents from being the XO. My duffle bags are mostly empty so I've got somewhere to put the rest of my gear on the flight home.

The bulk of what I'm taking home with me? Books, of course. My laptop stays with me in my assault pack, as does a broken-down hygiene bag. But all in all, I'm not carrying home that much stuff. The things that are going in the connex are things I can live without.

So when I get home, I'll be able to look at everything around me and ruthlessly throw things away. It's too much stuff. Too much clutter taking up space. Too many toys, too many orphaned keys or abandoned pens. This is the best time to clean house and start over.

Organizers say that if you haven't used it in a year, you probably don't need it. While I don't agree with that entirely, in my case, I do think that if I haven't missed it, I'll probably be able to throw it out.

So what's in your life that you can downsize or even get rid of? What can you change that will give you more time, more space, less to do? Because if I can essentially live out of a duffle bag, I bet you can cut some stuff from your life.

Try it. See what you come up with. You might surprise yourself.

Kill the Whore?
November 2, 2009

IN THEIR BOOK BEYOND Heaving Bosoms, Smart Bitches Sarah and Candy point out that more often than not, the whore stereotype is portrayed as a foil to the virtuous heroine. On my blog, I've pointed out multiple times that women in the Army who sleep around are remembered not for their job skills but for their reputation as whores. I can't speak to how women in the civilian world who are promiscuous are treated in the workplace as I have zero experience with civilian work places.

Here's my question: why is it that in fiction, women are not allowed to be promiscuous? They might have had sex before, but it is almost always off-stage and before the book opened. I just read a fantastic Tami Hoag novel where the slutty sister is brutally murdered by the serial killer (loved the book, mind you). The heroine and her sister caused me to do a lot of thinking.

The sister was not a bad person. She simply believed that since her stepfather began abusing her at thirteen that she really was born a whore and would never be anything more than a whore. A man loved her despite this, but her self-destructive behavior ultimately led to her death.

I truly felt bad for the sister. Despite her jealousy and her self-sacrifice (she drew the stepfather's attention away from her little sister), she was nevertheless killed for more or less being a whore. Tami's example of the whore with a heart of gold did not sugarcoat the fact that she was still a slut even if she was sympathetic.

Another greatly troubled female heroine is Starbuck on the new BattleStar Galactica. Starbuck believed, because of her mother's relentless demands and harsh punishments, that she was unworthy of love, to the point of running away screaming from the one man who could have loved her, despite it all. I love the character of Starbuck.

I recently read a chapter in a romance novel that I simply could not get past. The heroine was sleeping with a mark to gain knowledge for a man who was blackmailing her. Despite knowing the heroine was doing it because of blackmail, I could not get over the heroine in a romance novel having sex on the page with someone other than the hero.

So we've got a dichotomy out there. We want our heroines to be virtuous, even if they are not virgins. In fiction and in real life, we struggle with our women who are promiscuous and simply like sex. But at the heart of it, a woman in fiction is not allowed to like sex as much as a man. There are always consequences and this is the heart of the double standard.

We have the same challenge in the military. Women who sleep around are ridiculed, whereas men are ignored, at least until they are caught. It's not fair but it remains a fact of life. This is the same mentality that wants our women to be nurturers, yet wants to punish them for getting pregnant. We can't get ahead.

I'm not saying that we should embrace the whore mentality. South Park's episode, "Stupid Spoiled Whore" was a great portrayal of the pendulum swinging too far in the opposite direction. The portrayal of women in the media as sexy bimbos is self-destructive in and of itself and leads to even greater misogyny. And even as we move forward into the twenty-first century, I doubt that women's sexuality is going to be subject to any great changes. Easy women will continue to be mocked by the men who sleep with them and the whore will continue to be the foil for the virtuous heroine. What can we do to change this mentality and find a middle-of-the-road position that does not celebrate the whore but doesn't lynch her either.

Do you dare write a Starbuck? Can you write a heroine who is deeply troubled and uses sex as a method for seeking self-worth in male attention, yet still have a hero who loves her despite it all? Can this heroine be redeemed? Would you even want to or be able to write such a heroine? Why or why not?

Jessica Scott

Getting Off the Ledge
November 3, 2009

TODAY'S BLOG IS ABOUT perseverance. Today's blog is about not giving up when you're so damn frustrated you could scream. Today's blog is about the friends who keep you from hitting send when you really want to.

Becoming a writer has got to be one of the most frustrating experiences I've ever embarked on. The lows are so frequent in the beginning, it's really hard to find the energy to keep going. Even when you experience a personal triumph, the challenges still remain. They never end.

So what keeps me going?

Honestly, I have no idea. Well, there's the desire not to have my snazzy little MacBook go to waste. I feel like I have to get published simply because my dear husband bought me a MacBook prior to our deploying because I was going to be a writer.

But that's not really it. I've set this goal in my head (something to the effect of amounting to something in my life) and I've equated my future happiness with getting published and hopefully someday hitting the New York Times bestseller list (hopefully, this will still be relevant in the amount of time it's going to take me to get published, let alone make the list and hey, doesn't every author dream of hitting the Times?).

No, the real reason I keep going is because I have set a goal to sell a book and see it in print. It doesn't necessarily matter that I've told the world that I'm a

171

writer. In my mind, I'm not yet because I still haven't sold. And that hangs over my head like a ginormous blinking neon sign that says "Failure."

I've finished a book. I've actually written like ten books if you count the rewrites (which, truth be told, were completely new books at the end of it all). As I wait for my turn, I keep writing. I can't not write. I get insomnia, I get up and sit at the keyboard, editing, changing, writing. The ideas keep coming, too. It's as though I've created a crack in the wall and more ideas are coming faster than I can write.

So I'm going to keep getting after it, simply because I've set this goal for myself. I like writing. I like revisions, though I could probably use some good direction on that point, but I love seeing the raw idea take shape into something readable. I don't like rejection (honestly, who does?) but I try to use it to get better. What can I change? What am I not seeing? What still needs work?

I keep getting after it because I set a goal and I don't give up. Really. I don't. I might feel like it. I might take a knee every so often because the weight of keeping after it when you're the only one who believes in what you're doing can be really f**ng heavy sometimes. And maybe I still need a boatload more work. But I'll keep getting after it because I've had people tell me I suck before and I kept going after it. I didn't quit the basketball team in high school (though in that case, I probably should have—I really did suck at sports). Everyone told me to just give up but I didn't. Worth it? I have no idea, except that I set a goal and I had too much pride to quit.

It's hard getting up and seeing an empty inbox. It's hard getting up and waiting for the call. But the tiny boosts that come along the way from the people who help prop you up when you really want to lie down, make it worth it.

And I set a goal. It's either give up or keep getting after it. If it's all the same to you, I'll keep getting after it.

I've Stopped Reading...
November 4, 2009

...BOOKS THAT DON'T ENGAGE me. I've tried to stop reading critically. I've tried to get back into where I enjoy reading as a reader, not as a writer analyzing every word on the page to see what I like or don't. So when I have a book that I cannot put down, I literally find an excuse to carry it with me everywhere until I end up lying awake at two in the morning finishing it.

Even though I've stopped trying to pick apart books so I can sit back and enjoy the story, I know a book has lost me when I start skimming huge chunks. If I get to page two hundred and have no idea what I just read, it's really close to me putting a book aside. If I scan to the end just to find out what happened and that's all I care about, the book is a goner.

Because I've discovered so many authors this year that I absolutely adore (translation: will be going on a backlist glom as soon as I get home and can enjoy two-day free shipping), I have also discovered that when I'm just not engaged in a book, I simply won't finish it.

For myself, I want to really get pulled into a character's world and care about them, to the point that I will forego sleep to find out what comes next. I love Julie Kenner's Demon Hunting Soccer Mom series. I cannot wait to get home and pick up her next book, Torn, as well as the fifth Kate book. Julie world-builds in a way that has me forgetting that I'm reading a first person narrative and instead, I feel like I am living in the story. Her character's pain and laughter feels real to me.

Laura Kinsale (as you know if you've read this blog more than once) is another author who really pulls me in. Her characters are alive to me and their problems matter. Roxanne St. Claire's Bullet Catchers radiate sensuality, not raw sex, and I love a good sensual story packed with action. Allison Brennan is my go-to gal for suspense. Her stories hook me and I long ago gave up trying to figure out who done it and simply enjoy the ride with the characters.

These are examples of authors who I enjoy because of what I get from the story. If something jars me, I have enough faith in the author to pull me back in. Laura Griffin's Courtney Glass is one of the best wounded heroine's I've ever read. She's a train wreck and still I find myself rooting for her in the end. I've reread Whisper of Warning three times this year.

The point of this post is not to discuss which authors lose me but rather to figure out why? What went wrong that I was distracted from the outset and simply could not care about characters? In some cases, maybe it's a jarring personality that I could not get past. Or maybe I had reader expectations that were quickly stomped on and the book never recovered. Or it's an overuse of exclamation points in dialogue. What is it that makes me put the book down rather than keep reading to see if I reengage?

I can't tell you what goes wrong when I put a book down, I only know that I no longer feel like I'm committing a cardinal sin when I do. A book I might not like, someone else might love. My opinions, likes, and dislikes are my own and as I think about what went wrong in this book or that, I know that most likely, it's simply something I did not like. I try to identify why and what I might have done to change things, but mostly the author wrote a book a certain way because that's what the author felt needed to be written. I'm not going to criticize but I will try to learn from it.

But I won't necessarily finish it.

Tragedy at Fort Hood
November 6, 2009

I FOUND OUT ABOUT what happened yesterday at Fort Hood on Twitter. I couldn't access streaming video, so all I had for up-to-the-minute news was the constant stream on Twitter.

For everyone who passed on the relevant news, to include the requests for blood donations, thank you.

Fort Hood is my home. When I first followed my then-boyfriend (now dear husband) to Fort Hood almost eleven years ago, I was terrified. They'd just had a female gang leader arrested and court martialed. This was where I was going from my safe little base in Germany? This was where I was going to call home?

I found a small apartment outside the gate in Copperas Cove and got to know somewhere in the States other than my home in small-town central Maine. When a neighbor was shot a couple of buildings over in my apartment complex, first I was scared. This kind of thing didn't happen in Maine. Or in Germany. But when we realized that the woman was shot by a man she was involved with, it seemed less random and I moved on, without living in fear.

There are simple facts that most people who live at Fort Hood pay attention to. Don't live on Rancier. Stay away from certain clubs. Don't go down Rancier after dark.

But acts like what occurred yesterday bring an element of randomness into our lives once again. The shooting at Luby's in Killeen in the 90s was an act of randomness. The killings by Hasan (I will not call him by his rank) are a tragedy.

What I mean by the randomness is that we can't stop everyone. There were warning signs. Perhaps. Perhaps not. I truly believe our commanders make the best decisions they can with the information they have. Maybe mistakes were made and Hasan never should have been made to deploy. Maybe he should have been identified. I don't know and I will not speculate as to the information that his commanders had available. But I do know that if we let everyone who does not wish to deploy to Iraq or Afghanistan not deploy, we would not be able to do our mission. I would not be here if I had a choice, but it's my turn to be here, so that someone else gets to spend time with their family. This is what I signed up for, it is my responsibility and my duty.

We cannot live in fear that all Muslim soldiers will turn into a Hasan or an Akbar (the soldier who threw a grenade in his command tent) and turn on their fellow soldiers. We can listen and watch, and we can know what to do when bad things happen. The soldiers at the SRC reacted to the wounded immediately. More people might have died had they not reacted according to their training and immediately taken action to stop the bleeding. The first responders took him down.

The key to the resolution of the tragedy is training. Our soldiers were trained on how to deal with treating wounds in combat. They were trained on how to take out a shooter and control a crowd and secure a site. Our soldiers did this because they were trained.

We cannot stop a terrorist who is determined to blow himself up. We can, however, control how we react to these situations when they occur. We cannot give up our freedoms because someone wishes to do us harm. We can plan, prepare, and execute the mission when it happens.

What I'm getting at is last night on Twitter, while I was learning all I could and trying to responsibly retweet information and facts, I saw a lot of kneejerk reaction (some of which really pissed me off but that's another post). Gun control came up immediately. So did base security. So did the fact that Hasan is a Muslim. These are the kind of reactions that are to be expected. But let's take them for what they are and move forward.

All Muslims are not terrorists. All gun owners are not going to walk into a place and start shooting. The base security is what it is and oh, by the way, he did what thousands of us do every day when we go to work. We flash a badge and go on base. Searching every car is not only impractical, it doesn't make sense.

As we move forward, we must learn from this tragedy. Let's focus on what went right: our soldiers' reactions to what was essentially a combat situation. Let's learn from what could be done better in the future.

But let's not overreact and talk about taking away all guns or doing extra screenings on Muslims or whoever commits this week's act of random violence.

Bad things will happen. The question is not how to stop them (though we should take actions where we can), but how to react to them. Because being prepared to react will minimize the casualties and will help us maintain the free society that makes us great.

My thoughts and prayers are with the families of the victims. If you have not already done so, please donate blood, wherever you are in the world, because someone always needs it.

Missing the Zoo
November 8, 2009

I'M NOT TALKING ABOUT the kids, either, though you might have assumed I was from the title. I'm talking about missing the family menagerie.

I miss my pets. I miss Lilly (the hundred-plus pound lab/lap dog) and the way she absolutely destroys everything in the backyard. I miss my crazy-ass cat Cookie who manages to sit on my lap despite the laptop. I miss Ms. Megan, our first puppy who hid under the couch and is the reason we had to get Robbie and then, after he died, Lilly.

Ms. Megan has anxiety issues. When she was a puppy, she hated being alone. The neighbors said she would howl all day long until we got home. We ended up getting her her own puppy and she was perfectly happy afterwards. When Robbie was cruelly murdered (yes, he was actually murdered by some sick bastard who fed him antifreeze-laced meat), Ms. Megan went crazy once more. Six months out from deploying to Iraq, we started searching for another dog. It was either that or put her on anxiety meds. We opted for another dog.

Lilly fit in instantly, though we suspected she might have been part greyhound because she was so skinny. Anyone who's ever had a lab knows that didn't last long. By the time we'd left her at my in-law's house, she was pushing ninety pounds. Thanks to my in-laws spoiling her, the damn dog has topped 105 lbs and is still growing.

And I'm grateful. I'm grateful that my husband's parents took in our two dogs once again for over a year and treated them like their own (but seriously, the dogs are getting their feelings hurt: they are not sleeping on my furniture!). I'm grateful that my brother-in-law took two cats into his home and kept them well-fed and happy (though Cookie is a little upset at the lack of hard liquor but that's another post for another time).

I'm also glad that my mom got another dog this year because the thing my kids missed the most about going to Grammy's (other than Mommy and Daddy of course) was all their pets. My kids have grown up in a zoo. Having a dog that's taller than your head has probably impacted them but mostly in a good way. My kids love their animals and are really looking forward to rounding everyone up and driving home.

Over here in Iraq, there are no unit mascots (at least not on our base). I got in trouble for leaving milk out that a stray cat (who was incidentally incredibly friendly) happened to drink because we're not supposed to feed the vectors. Strays are called vectors because they're not vaccinated and can carry a whole slew of diseases harmful to soldiers.

Despite living out of a duffle bag and having to walk to the showers, the thing I missed the most (besides the kids) was having a cat sleeping on my head, licking the pillow and purring in my ear. I miss the sound of claws on the wood floor. I don't miss the rabbit-sized hairballs but I'll live. I miss the constant sense of well-being, surrounded by my animals and my kids. The noise and clutter that makes a house a home or in my case a zoo. So as we get ready to get out of here, it's not just a home I'm heading back to. I'm going back to life as usual, with the hassle, the noise, and the absolute adoration of the household pets.

I'll be busy, but I can't wait.

Historical Subversion in Romance
November 9, 2009

WE IN ROMANCE HAVE a unique power as writers. We write characters for women who dare to step outside the norm. We have characters who defy convention and do what's right, regardless of what people think.

We as a society have a different problem right now. In Richmond, California, a crowd of onlookers stood by and participated in the gang-rape of a young woman. No one called police. No one tried to stop it. No one alerted the teachers.

No one acted, and the reigning theory is the fear of what the mob might do or think stopped people.

It's damn hard to stand up to a crowd of people and try to stop something. It's damn hard to stand up and say "this is wrong," or "I don't care what you think." Think of the scandal. The whole crowd might have called you names or turned on you or worse. So you sold your soul and remained quiet while evil had its way once more.

Something happens to our daughters as they grow up. As children, they play and have a grand old time and have opinions, but as they transition from tweens to teenagers, social pressure plays an even bigger role on our daughters than our sons. By that I mean that our girls are expected to be cute and smart and popular and honestly, who doesn't envy the head cheerleader when she gets to date the basketball team captain?

I won't even lie: my teenage years were spent buried in books reading about women who dared defy convention and marry who they wanted, damn the scandal. That's a pretty powerful thought. Damn what people think about you. Damn what society expects of you. Damn what your parents expect if it's not going to make you happy. One of the greatest gifts my mom ever gave me was to raise me with the knowledge that whatever I decided to do, she'd support me so long as I was happy. I found out later in life that my dad thought I should be a lawyer but that was long after I'd already joined the Army.

Now, that's not to say that my folks didn't have some heartburn about me joining up. I was eighteen years old, overweight, and an average student who sucked at sports and worked at McDonalds. But I joined anyway and they were there to kiss me goodbye and tell me they loved me, no matter that I was going to wear fatigues to work for the next few years.

But I digress. The whole point of that tangent was to point out that even though I had some pretty strong social fitting-in issues, my folks supported me in doing what I wanted. A lot of women today don't have that. I see moms pushing their daughters to have plastic surgery or daughters pushing for it because it will make them pretty and therefore popular.

In a romance novel, particularly historicals, the heroine defies conventions in some way. She either ends up in an unconventional situation, like Maddy in Flowers from the Storm who is incredibly stubborn, or like Jocilyn in Savage Thunder, who falls in love with a man who's half Native American, half white. Both characters thumb their nose at what society expects and both have some pretty powerful societal influence pushing them to conform.

The first time I picked up a historical over here, I rolled my eyes and thought: great another girl trying to get married.

Why, I wondered, was scandal such a big deal? I mean, honestly, as a female in the military, I've had plenty of rumors started about me, to include the pinnacle of my deployment, making the latrine wall. When I was younger, they used to really bother me but I learned quickly that not only can you not stop rumors, you'll just lose sleep over them if you let them get to you. So to me, I'm like really? Scandal and rumors are a big deal?

Well, yeah, they are.

The refusal to conform is a testament to the romance heroines' subversive power. They do the right thing, even when society says not to. The romance heroine would pick up the phone and try to stop the rape that occurred outside a high school rather than worry about what the crowd thought.

Maybe romance is a good thing for our daughters to read, to try and find a way to stand up to the crowd and what the popular kids are doing, and dare to find their own way in the world.

Conflicted About Fort Hood Memorial
November 10, 2009

I WAS UNABLE TO watch the Hood memorial ceremony from over here in Iraq but I caught a bit of it on TV.

I've got to say, having sat through multiple memorials over here, watching the TV for the one at Hood felt a little off. It was so strange seeing the field that I run PT on every morning filled with soldiers, the American flag draped over the entrance of the III Corps Headquarters.

The first memorial I ever went to was for a battalion commander we lost here in combat. It was a horrible shock and a catastrophic event. The CAC, where we conduct all ceremonies here on the FOB, was packed. After all, Lieutenant Colonels don't usually make the casualty roster. So when my battalion lost a private and the CAC wasn't nearly as full, it was kind of an eye opener.

I appreciate that the president went and offered his respects at the ceremony. But I wonder, did he ask the family members if they wanted him there? And I'm truly just wondering that. I thought he made a thoughtful decision earlier this year when he left the decision of photographs being taken at Dover up to the families. But I really wonder if anyone asked these families at Fort Hood. They are as much a casualty of this war as anyone who died over here this year.

On the other hand, I recognize that the nation needs to mourn with us. That there is a kinship and a support for our soldiers even when we might close ranks and only stand with those who serve with us, those who know what it feels like to stand on a tarmac and salute a flag-draped coffin. That is an experience very few Americans know or understand and the reaction is to keep it to ourselves.

When we put on the uniform, we choose to become symbols of our nation. We give up our rights as individuals and become Soldier. That does not mean our deaths should be impersonal or turned into a symbol. Because each one of those Soldiers being mourned today was a brother or a sister, a son or a daughter, a wife or a husband.

So I'm conflicted. My gut says this is ours but my head says we need to show the world that we're better than what that bastard tried to make us out to be.

My heart and prayers go out to the families of the victims and to the victims still recovering. Get well, get strong, we still need you.

The person, not the symbol.

Veterans Day Thoughts From Iraq
November 11, 2009

I FINISHED READING DAVID Finkel's The Good Soldiers earlier this week. I was impacted. I could visualize the battalion commander and the private equally. I felt their pain when they sat in the chapel and paid tribute to their fallen brothers.

I can't really describe all the emotions this book brought to the surface. I look at the portraits that Finkel created and I can see those men in the faces of soldiers I see around me every day. I look at the battalion commander in the book more than anything as a man first, a commander second. I can see the dichotomy in the men and women around me.

Mr. Finkel created a book that impacted me in a way that a nonfiction book rarely does. I could not put this book down. I cringed when the bombs exploded. I could feel the commander's pain when he visited the wounded.

Though I have been a veteran for the last fourteen years, this year I become a combat veteran. I know the sound of incoming mortar fire. I know the fear of sitting in an intersection as an Iraq vehicle comes down the road and the pressure that tightens around my chest in uncertainty. I know the sound of the M4 going off inside the TOC and the absolute, instant grief of thinking you've lost a good friend. I have felt the blast of a thousand pound bomb a quarter mile away. The sound of the air weapons team over head is a comfort, not an annoyance. The thunder of the 50 cal in the test fire pit against my ribs is reassuring. The sounds of my soldiers around me is a sign that we are doing what we are meant to do. Protect and defend.

There is a bond between soldiers but the bond I feel toward the soldiers in my company will never diminish. We will sit back and laugh in the next years as we see each other in the PX or at the PT track. This is my company, these are my soldiers. Every soldier in my brigade can call home because of what my Signal soldiers bring to the mission.

The tradition and the history in the Army is a source of comfort. I know now why the veterans seek out the Officer's Club for one more taste of the brotherhood we share. I know I will be back in Iraq again in two years. Or if not here, Afghanistan. I choose to serve because this is what I know, this is what I do, and this is what I love. My journey as a writer has been fulfilling and challenging but nothing compares to the feel of firing a 50 cal for the first time, or the confidence of knowing I can hit what I aim at.

Each of us volunteered to be in the Army. If we stay, we volunteer to continue to serve. My fellow sisters-in-arms at the RomVets paved the way to allow me to be a signaler, a combat medic, a military police officer. I serve today because they proved I could.

To all the soldiers who came before me, I thank you.

Beauty Lessons From Iraq
November 12, 2009

I HAD AN INTERESTING Twitter conversation last night with Deidre Knight. We started talking about makeup and I commented that I've forgotten how to wear makeup. We discovered that we both love Bobbi Brown cosmetics and that my first stop before I am allowed to take leave is taking my credit card and my face to visit the Bobbi Brown in Saks in Austin.

But over here in Iraq, my makeup has been redefined as minimalist if not nonexistent. But when I get home, oh yeah, the makeup bag is coming out. I'm wearing foundation—well, tinted moisturizer—to work. And eye shadow. Probably a little blush. I want to look and feel like a woman when I get home and to be honest, I've forgotten how.

Oh, I remember how to apply a little blush, but I can't look in the mirror here without feeling like it's too much. When I have worn a little eyeliner over here, I look in the mirror and think it's too thick. So I need a professional intervention to teach me how to wear makeup again. How to dress like a woman, how not to talk like an infantryman in everyday conversation.

I'm not just coming home, I'm readjusting to being in another country. I've never been around a lot of civilians, so when I go to RWA, I'm going to need to adjust to being around that many fabulous women again.

But as far as beauty in Iraq, there have been certain things I could not live without. I don't have the ability to try things out. I purchase what I know works. So here's the list of stuff I wouldn't have made it through Iraq without, and yes, this list is 100% superficial and girly and unimportant in the grand scheme of fighting the war.

10. Clinique Long Wear mascara. Doesn't come off, even in sweat and 115 degree heat.

9. MAC Longwearing eyeliner pencil. That stuff goes on easy, doesn't melt off and doesn't smear. It's there for the day.

8. TNS Recovery Complex. The only serum I've found that really, really works. The lines around my eyes are much less pronounced than they were when we got here.

7. Laura Mercier Flawless Skin Moisturizer. This stuff is a godsend. My skin feels plump and dewy

and it's so rich and luxurious, a hard thing to maintain in this arid desert.

6. Clinique SPF 15 Lipgloss in First Blush. A nude color that provides SPF (a must) and just a hint of gloss. No color, just moisture.

5. Clinique Daily Defense SPF 25. I've stood on a flight line for 6 hours and not gotten a sunburn.

4. Skin Medica Vitalize Peel. I know you're supposed to have a doctor do this but this chemical peel is easy to do yourself (I'm not recommending you try this at home, so don't blame me if you burn your skin). But this peel is fantastic and you can get it on eBay dirt cheap compared to having a doc do it. My skin feels incredible after the peel and it's evened out my sun damage.

3. Laura Mercier Cleansing Oil and Tonic Water. I love this set. The oil cleans without drying and the tonic feels like it could be its own moisturizer. Love this stuff.

2. L'Occitane Shea Butter Hand Cream. Need I say more? This stuff is fantastic, smells clean, and keeps my hands silky smooth all day long.

1. Bumble and Bumble Gentle Shampoo and Super Rich Conditioner. I was using stuff that cost twice as much but my hair still felt like coarse straw. Now, I rinse with cold water and use this product every day and my hair feels amazing, even after not having a hair cut for over 6 months. This stuff is worth the price and has my loyalty forever!

Beauty in Iraq is much more pared down than in the States. I don't wish to stand out but I still like to feel like a girl. These products were the best I found to get through the year and even though I'm going home, I feel like these products are going to remain in the rotation.

The War Finally Hit Home
November 13, 2009

IN THE NINE YEARS our Army has been at war, I've been incredibly lucky. I've known people who have been killed but they haven't been one of mine. My husband has lost soldiers, my soldiers have lost friends and spouses, but my soldiers and my friends have been spared. Even the shootings at Fort Hood, where my home was violated by that son of a bitch, felt strangely detached because I wasn't there.

Monday, a good friend of mine collapsed and was sent to the CSH. I'd just been reading the brigade newsletter, looking over the faces of the men and women we lost this year and my husband called to tell me about our mutual friend. The grief was instant and overwhelming and we knew nothing other than he was in the CSH.

Thank God he's fine. But I was reading the Stars and Stripes tonight and I just found out one of my former troops died in Afghanistan this week. I remember this soldier and the team we were part of like I'd just seen him yesterday. The night we'd stayed up in the node center and he'd sworn there was a DC power cable to the management shelter (there wasn't). The night we sent him looking for chem light batteries. Or the day of September 11 when we couldn't find him and he'd just bought civilian clothes the day prior and we'd all thought he was part of whatever was going on.

He was a crazy kid who'd wanted nothing more than to be a combat arms soldier but instead he was a signal soldier. Looks like he got his wish and made it to the infantry. He never owned any civvies until a year after he'd been in the regular Army. He'd sit in his room and write music, content to just be on his own. There was the time he put a CD in the node center's work station and crashed the whole system. I smoked the living shit out of him that day.

It's weird because these are the things I remember about my team that Dale was a part of. He was a good kid and a good sport and, God, did we laugh back then. My node center wasn't the best or the fastest but we were close knit. We've all gone our separate ways since then but I remember my platoon.

The war hit home today and even though it's been half a decade or more since I've seen any of my old team, I remember them well. And Dale's death has hit me harder than I thought the loss of a soldier I haven't seen in years would.

This fucking sucks. I hate the war. I hate this place. I want everyone to come home. And I'm tired of reading the names in the bottom of a newspaper somewhere knowing that somewhere, someone is mourning.

Tonight, that someone is me.

Jessica Scott

Out of Order, Chaos
November 13, 2009

I'VE LEARNED A LOT of things about myself this year in Iraq, but one thing stands out to me: I am very much a creature of habit. I think I border on the edge of OCD, and I'm not being a smart-ass when I say that. Most of the time, I'm incredibly scatterbrained. I don't remember where I put things and my filing system is...well, let's just say that if I die, I hope my husband can figure out our finances.

I have to work extra hard to keep my life from falling apart. When my oldest daughter was born, I decided I needed a key-holder by the door. I don't even think about it. I come in the house and hang my keys. Every single time. So there's a little bit of panic when I look and they're not there.

I do the same thing here. I have my eye protection in a side pouch of my assault pack. In the morning, I change to the sunglasses, at night to the clear lenses. But the case is always in the same place. My iPod is in my front left pocket. It's reassuring to me to reach up and know it's there and when it isn't, I stop and have to remember where it is so that I know it's not lost.

I asked my husband where something was this morning and he made a joke to the effect of "color me surprised, you don't know where something is." But we've moved. So where I was keeping something for the whole year is no longer where it is right now. When it's not in its place, I can't find it. In applying this to my writing, I'm very much the same. I sit in my bed, my desk lap on my thighs, my MacBook on my desk with its sad little broken Apple light. I keep my files organized, at least to me. My books are all in the Books file. Each series has its own folder. I have to do it this way, otherwise I can never find a damn thing. Soldiers think it's anal when the Command Sergeant Major says that all first aid pouches will be worn in the exact same spot on every soldier. This makes sense, though, because in combat, you need to react, not search for something, and if it's in the same place, everyone knows.

I am going quietly insane right now because I can't find the charging plug for my iPod. I moved it, in that I took it to my CHU last night as I knew I was not going to write, but take a night off and recharge my brain. I tweeted. I surfed. I vegged out.

I lost my cable. I left it in the same place for a year and now I can't find it because I moved it. I remember the last time I saw it but after that, it's like a fugue state where I have no idea where it went. This is what happens when I break the pattern. This is what happens when everything is not in its place.

I'll find it, as soon as I buy a new one (say a prayer that the PX has one or I'm really in trouble). But how far over the edge am I that I have these rituals and routines that ease my mind? I work in chaos all the time but if I know where something is, even if the location is on a calendar somewhere, I can cope. I can handle all kinds of things at once, but I react very poorly to being blindsided, which is the equivalent of moving my cable.

I can thrive in chaos but require order. I'm the worst at organizing but I can hold all the facts. One of the hardest things for me to learn how to do was organize my storylines and keep the plot moving forward in a coherent arc. I know I have more to learn about writing and about the Army but finding a place to put everything is an important, difficult habit to enforce.

The Published Panacea
November 14, 2009

THE ARMY HAS TAUGHT ME that whatever I put my mind to, I can achieve. I decided I was going to be a published writer but everywhere I turn, roadblocks continue to pop up. See, publishing is only partially about what I can do. Now, I'll be the first one to tell you, when I went through the first round of agent hunting in 2008, I soundly deserved to be rejected. I might not have known it at the time, but what I was sending out was hot garbage. I had a good query letter but the work itself was...well, it never should have gone out. Ever.

Fast forward to now. I haven't submitted a query since late 2008, before I deployed to Iraq. A few months afterward, my agent picked me up and I was off to the races. Or so I thought. I kept writing, and writing kept me sane over here. I was able to put a whole lot of emotions and time and energy into the seven books I've written or rewritten this year. I learned how to critique my own manuscript, or, at least, I'm a hell of a lot better about it than I used to be, though I'm sure I still have more work to do.

But I've decided that I'm going to be published. Can I really control that? My books are military romance, but it seems like there's only one author out there who writes novels about military characters that are not romantic suspense. My stuff is not romantic suspense, so where does that leave me? And what happens if I don't get published? What does that mean to me as a writer and as a person who has not succeeded at whatever I've tried before?

I'm pretty sure the book is as good as I can get it right now. I've written a book that doesn't have the parts I skip in other books. There isn't a secondary romance because I tend to skip those. The plot centers on the two characters' emotional journey. The great Kate Duffy told me once that the characters in another project of mine were not handling things better than real people did. Maybe that's part of my challenge in finding a place to fit. My book—and all my books—reflect the life that soldiers around me experience. So they're not as uplifting or light-hearted as a normal romance.

Maybe there isn't a market for a book that spends the first half in a hospital room at Fort Hood. That is a distinct possibility and a chance that I may have to shelve this book and move on to something else. But that's the problem. I don't want to give up on these characters. I don't want people to not get a chance to see a glimpse of life inside the military and a character who chooses to stay in the Army as opposed to getting out. Because that's who I'm surrounded by. Men and women who choose to serve, despite the challenges the military life demands of them.

Maybe I'm not writing romance. I'm not sure. I know these books are not what Bob Mayer calls "fictional memoirs." They are not me put on paper. But what does it mean to me if I never see my name in print? Does it mean that I just didn't try hard enough? Does it mean that I'm writing what the publishing world does not want?

I'm not sure. I know I'm at a crossroads in my life right now. I'm getting ready to go through a huge transition period coming home from Iraq and taking my family back. I know my writing is something I can't not do, but maybe I'll need to set it aside for a time and figure out why I really want to be published. What am I really hoping to gain? Does it make me a better person, a better mom or wife? Does it make the laundry get done faster?

This isn't about the cruel literary world not taking me on. This is about me finding my place in it. Maybe I need to do more work and make my manuscript better. If that's the case, I'll eventually figure it out and write another book. Maybe my military series has no place. If that's the case, I'll whip my paranormal apocalyptic into shape and start submitting that.

But I need to find a way to let go of the crushing disappointment each time another "not right for me" comes back. This is not a rejection of me as a person.

This is not, necessarily, a rejection of my book. It is a statement as to salability and personal tastes.

I'm still me. I'm still stuck in Iraq. I'm still a mom of two healthy girls and a wife to a great, loving husband. The pass on my novel is not—and should not—be a soul crushing defeat. So I'll figure out a way through it. And—though I hope this is not the case—if all the agents who currently have War's Darkest Fear pass, I'll start revising the next project.

Because the stories are still in my brain, still leaking out onto the page, demanding to be heard.

Everything Hurts
November 15, 2009

I'M NOT SURE WHY I'm reacting like this today. I'm stuck. I'm stuck in Iraq, I'm stuck in my writing career. I'm a constant movement forward person. I'm always in motion and today I'm stuck.

Last night on the webcam, my three year old crossed her arms and dropped her little head and all I wanted to do was hold her and feel her breath on my neck. I wanted to brush my five year old's hair from her face and listen to her tell me how she learned what a veteran was in school the other day. I want the aggravation of getting them to bed on time and the hugs and kisses first thing in the morning. I want it so goddamned bad and there is nothing I can do to make the time go by faster.

My soul aches with how badly I want to go home now. Sure, life is simpler here in Iraq but damn, it's not worth it. I've avoided everything that hurts, everything that gets too much emotion for the last year because if I let it out, it feels like I'll never stop. I don't watch violence on TV, I can't stand to hear a baby cry. Today, everything is leaking out and I can't put it away. I don't know why. My kids have cried on the phone before.

The same uncertainty with going home is tearing me up. I'm putting on a brave face for all the soldiers but the possibility of staying through Christmas makes my soul bleed. We're here for the team and if we have to stay, then we have to stay, but that doesn't make the disappointment any easier.

What I've Learned This Year
November 16, 2009

JUST WANTED TO POP on and say thank you for the emails and the support. Today was a rough one for some reason and I thought I'd be honest on the blog about the pain I was feeling missing my kids. I mean, that's what I'm really going through as a mom, so...

It's not all bad though. I've learned a lot this year and accomplished a lot more. So in the effort of dragging my depressing self out of the gulley of "what the heck have I done," I'm going to figure out everything that I have managed to accomplish this year, both Army and writing.

Army:

Got rated best platoon leader out of eleven in the battalion. I was shocked but thought that was pretty cool. My battalion commander listens to me now, as opposed to thinking I'm just a mouthy lieutenant.

Was selected to be my company executive officer (second in command) early. Fixed the property book so that we have 100% accuracy of everything we own (trust me this is harder than it seems).

Have re-motivated my supply sergeant. There is nothing better in the Army than taking a kid who's struggling and turning him around. My supply sergeant went from being thought of as the worst in the battalion to the best. As a team, we've still got room to grow, but he's come a long way and I just smile when he starts talking smack about how squared away he is, because he deserves it.

Got selected for captain. Okay, stop laughing. We all know that getting promoted to captain these days just requires a pulse but I thought I'd throw it in for a laugh.

Grew a lot as a leader. Had some serious challenges but I think I've learned a lot about myself and my own weaknesses and strengths as an officer.

Writing:

When I left for Iraq, I had two books done and a third halfway. Now, I've got seven completed but I've rewritten four of them so in reality, I wrote eleven books this year.

Have grown my blog. When I started the year, I had ten hits a week. Now, I'm up to almost two thousand, so thank you, everyone who stops by the site and says hi or just checks up on me.

Hooked up with some fab mentors and an awesome critique partner. Can't wait to read more and continue to grow.

Learned from a great agent. Things might not have worked out but I'm still exceptionally grateful that she took me on.

Was mentioned on Smart Bitches and Romancing the Blog (and still smile when I think about it, so thank you, SBSarah and Sarah!).

This year has been full of ups and downs, and the roller coaster is about to get even more crazy before we get out of here. Thank you for everyone who's supported me, sent care packages or a kind email. Hopefully, I'll have a fab new agent soon and will get my head straightened out and focused back on my goals, which are be a kick-ass Army officer and a published author.

No more bummer posts. I'm coming home soon!!

The Evolving Editor
November 17, 2009

SO I'VE WRITTEN A lot this year, right? People might think it's a little insane to have written or rewritten eleven books in a year but they are all basically firsts, except for the three that I chunked and rewrote and I'm not sure how to characterize them.

But what I have learned is that I've got a technique now for revising that I did not have at the beginning of the year. So onward to the object lesson.

I wrote The Last Sunrise in February-March timeframe. My first foray into paranormal (good versus evil and the Book of Revelations, along with a couple of sexy almost-fallen angels) and I really loved the idea. But, when I finished it in February, I put it away. I wrote a query for it and tucked it into my Books file.

At some point in September, I pulled it back out and read through it in Word. I have learned a new trick that works for me, in that I write in Scrivener but I edit almost exclusively in Word. I have no idea why it works but it seems to so I'm sticking with it for now.

Anyway, read through it and chunked about two-thirds of the novel and once more, started over, including the opening scene that I loved. Finished the new draft, which is now titled Resurrection (yes this happens in the book and both my mom and my aunt are going to disown me for the blasphemy) and once more, put it away.

Except I didn't. I finished it about three weeks ago and have now opened the Word document today and started revising. While the essential plot remains the same, the revisions are pretty extensive layering, smoothing, and tightening. One thing the Army has taught me that I'm now able to see in my writing is that just because something makes sense to me, doesn't mean it came out that clear. I see that in my sentences now and have started working to smooth them out.

So I've learned something about myself. I have to write a complete first draft to figure out what the story actually is. Then write that book. Then revise and clean up. Thankfully, of the seven books I've got written, four are in the second round of edits right now, so with any luck, when I finally do get around to revising, the drafts are cleaner, tighter and don't involve massive deleting of texts.

Will You Read My Manuscript?
November 20, 2009

I DEBATED LONG AND hard about posting this for two reasons: one, I am not a published author and have no idea the time constraints that published authors find themselves under. Nor have I experienced a raving email from someone I said no to or gotten a nasty response for a harsh critique. So

I'm only writing this from what I've observed, not from what I've experienced.

There's been a lot floating around the interweb about what a pain it is to be asked to read someone's manuscript. Most published authors I know or have spoken to about this cite either a fear of being accused of stealing someone's work or legal reasons from their publishers.

There are, however, other reasons and one of the main ones was that most often, some published authors think that unpublished authors are simply trying to skirt the system and get a referral to an agent or an editor. While I may not truly understand the sheer numbers of people like this, I wonder if that is truly what people are looking for when they ask a published author to read their manuscript.

Now, I'll be the first to admit that being handed a manuscript beneath the bathroom stall is both rude and awkward and reeks of desperation on the part of the writer. But assuming that newbie writers should know better is a false assumption, even if they should have some basic social understanding of etiquette in general. I've been "a writer" for almost two years now and there is beyond too much information that I don't know. I did not know about the Miss Snark website until last summer, after I queried half the agents in the business.

Disclaimer: I have asked published authors to read my book. I sent an email and asked. And you know what? Most said I can't and I was perfectly fine with that. I understand that people are busy. I understand that reading someone's work who needs a ton of editing can be exceptionally challenging on both patience and brain power. I know this because I have pushed a book that was in no way shape or form ready to be read by anyone other than my cat.

I will also say now, thank you to the authors who did say yes, even if it was to read a few pages and say something like, "I think you have talent but I don't think this book is going to get you published."

Here's the thing I love about the writers I have had the good fortune to interact with. Even if they haven't read my manuscript, they're still a source of inspiration and mentorship. Writers mentor better than any group I know of, including Army officers. So I am well and truly grateful for the writers who have taken me under their wing. I know I am incredibly fortunate to have their support and their brains to pick on all matters from depression to the writing industry to what to look for in an agent.

I am grateful to the writers who declined as well because I learned not only how to do so with grace but also that once published, the demands you have as a writer increase. When I asked one author why her publisher had a policy against reading uncontracted books, she was gracious enough to explain to me the whys behind the decision so that I now know that too many writers have experienced being accused of stealing someone's idea. I am grateful because she took the time to explain something to me that I didn't know.

I recognize that every published author cannot help every unpublished author. But when did it become the de facto sentiment to be so irritated that someone asked you to read something they wrote? Now, I understand being irritated if they're simply trying to circumvent the system. And I understand how hard it is when people put you on the spot. I also fully understand that there are going to be those screaming emails when you do politely tell someone no and they lose their minds on you, blaming you for everything.

Agents go through it every day. I'm willing to bet that every agent in the business has sent a rejection only to get blasted by some unprofessional writer who blames them for not believing in their project that almost certainly would be a NYT bestseller if only someone would pick them out of the slush pile. This behavior is wrong. Agents should not be subjected to it and neither should published authors. It is not your responsibility to help me make my manuscript better. It is mine to learn. But part of that learning involves asking questions.

So unpublished writers, approach published writers or agents on Facebook or Twitter with an idea of what you are asking. It takes time to read a manuscript, time most published authors will tell you they just don't have. If someone does take the time to read and offer comments, don't argue. Listen and learn what you can. I'm not telling you not to ask, but don't email every published author and ask. Be nice and if they say no, say "thank you" anyway.

But published authors, please remember that someone somewhere along the way helped you, taught you or mentored you and while you can't help everyone, if you can, please do so, even knowing that it is not your job. No one has a responsibility to do anything to help anyone else out.

That doesn't mean you can't.

I know it's frustrating and time-consuming, but please try not to be aggravated with us. Just like many of you are irritated with Harlequin Horizons for taking advantage of unpublished or newbie writers' ignorance and desperation, please remember what it feels like to want to see your book in print so badly, you'd do anything, yes even hand a complete stranger a manuscript beneath the latrine wall. Yes, the onus is on us to work for it, and keep working for it. But if you can take a few minutes, even if it's only reading ten pages of a manuscript and offering pointers, please do.

And unpublished writers, be grateful for what you get. I'm not saying you should lick boots or anything like that, but remember that other people's time is precious to them so figure out what you need, be specific when you ask, and be okay with being told no. If you really want to be a writer, you'd better get used to it, because being told no is standard issue in the writing world and you'll hear a lot of it. But every so often, you'll get a yes in there, so be grateful when you get one.

This post, hopefully, expresses just how truly grateful I am to the published writers who have helped me or simply offered a kind word when I needed one. This post also, hopefully, reminds all of us that no one is an island and that if at all possible, you should pay it forward when you can.

My Idea!
November 22, 2009

I'VE WRITTEN BEFORE ABOUT finding my own work in someone else's. I wrote about it recently upon discovering that one of the soldiers in David Finkel's The Good Soldiers was seeing a little girl every time he closed his eyes and that I have a character who, though he predates my reading of The Good Soldiers, had a similar issue.

In February, I wrote the book that was then titled The Last Sunrise, about a special operations team trying to prevent the real Biblical Apocalypse. Great idea, right? Well, I just rewrote the book and it has key players from the hosts of heaven as well as the fallen angels.

Jamming so far, right?

Then I pick up a fantastic book and go "oh shit." Love the book. Will read the entire series when I get home and have bookstore access. But now, as I edit my draft, I'm looking for ways to differentiate my story from this one. It's not even that similar, other than the fact that we're both using names from religious history, such as Belial and Lilith.

But I worry about it. Just like I pitched a book to JoAnn Ross's agent that had the same name and same central issue without knowing about her book, I'm worried now that I'm going to look like I'm biting off this other author.

I know there's nothing new under the sun. I know that no works are created in a void, but why does this same thing seem to keep happening to me? Am I over-worried about something that I truly cannot control, especially if I'm pulling from the collective unconscious of the world?

Because that's truly what I feel I do. As a writer, I'm tapped into something that demands my fingers move on the keyboard. The characters become people in my head and I know them. I hear their dialogue and jot it down as fast as I can because if I don't, it hounds me until I do.

Then I discover the same impulse has already established itself somewhere else. But just like Madagascar and The Wild came out at the same time, I don't think anyone can say this is a copy, because it's not. My books were written before I even knew about this series.

But I know that as I continue with my own books, I'm going to have to consciously differentiate my world from this other author's world, as opposed to trusting my impulse from the collective unconscious.

What about you? Have you discovered your story matches something similar to someone else's? What did you do about it, if anything?

An Odd Mix of Emotions
November 26, 2009

YOU WOULDN'T THINK THAT being in Iraq, there would be much to be thankful for. On the other hand, you might think I have a lot to be thankful for.

I'm on the side of the latter. I have a ton to be thankful for today and while I'm not going to bore you with the details, I will say that like Memorial Day, I had a lot of strong emotions that I couldn't figure out where they were coming from. We were in the chow hall, and our DFAC puts on quite a display. There were tablecloths and decorations and bottles of sparkling wine everywhere. It was really great. But in the midst of it all, in the middle of hearing everyone wish each other Happy Thanksgiving, there was a knot in the middle of my chest.

I don't know why. I have so much to be grateful for, not the least of which is the fact that I was sitting at the table with my husband. I mean, you can't ask for more than that. But the knot was there and I had a hell of a time stomping it down. It's been on the edge of breaking through all day and I don't know why.

My daughters are safe and happy and healthy, along with my mom. I've got the most amazing friends and mentors in the writing community and in my personal life. There is no indirect fire today. My soldiers are safe, a few days from getting out of here. Sitting over here on the FOB, seeing the Colonel and the Command Sergeant Major and everyone walking through the chow hall wishing everyone Happy Thanksgiving, I should have felt relief. I should have felt happiness to be sitting near my husband and knowing I'll sleep tonight in a bed next to him.

So I'm not going to complain, only state that there is a knot that I don't know the origin of and I cannot name. I refuse to dwell on it. I refuse to be anything less than incredibly grateful for the blessings in my life and the lessons that I've learned this year. Most of them were difficult pills to swallow, but in the end they made me stronger.

I don't know what the coming year will bring. I only know that today, I am grateful for so much.

What Is It Like?
November 30, 2009

WHAT IS IT LIKE to stand on the airfield at a ramp ceremony? What is it like when there's a mortar attack? How many casualties did you take this year?

I've had my cherry popped in more ways than one this year but being asked these questions was a milestone I didn't want to see breached. I flew on a Black Hawk for the first time, fired an AK-47, and felt an earthquake. I stood in my CHU as indirect fire hit our base.

But I didn't want to talk about what it's like when someone dies. One of the new lieutenants asked me how many casualties we took this year. I didn't want to give him a number, I wanted to tell him about the names. The brothers and sisters that we lost. The husbands and wives and sons and daughters.

And now I know how others felt when I asked the questions he put to me. Awkward. Unsure. Irritated. Saddened.

But I gave him the number, hoping he would catch on that I didn't want to talk about it. He didn't. He asked about the worst day. I told him there were two for me but many more for each soldier in the brigade. The day we lost a battalion commander in a catastrophic blast. I'll never forget the heavy shock that settled over my shoulders when my boss told me that Warhorse 6 was hit. I wasn't close to him, but he'd taken time to chew me out several times when I was the brigade signal officer and I respected him. He talked trash to me at a test fire range in Kuwait and I gave it right back. I don't think he expected a female LT to smart off but then again, he didn't so much as blink. His sergeant major laughed.

The next hard day struck my then-new company hard. One of our soldiers was married to a girl who was hit by a mortar. When I explained this to the new lieutenant, he was shocked. How does someone get hit by a mortar? "Wrong place, wrong time?" he asked. No. Just being in Iraq. My husband took her death hard as he worked with her. I took her death hard because I worked with her husband, and my heart broke for him.

But then the LT crossed the barrier. He asked about the ramp ceremony. I've written about them, but nothing on earth will prepare you to stand at

212

attention, holding a salute you would rather die than drop and see a flag-draped coffin carried on to the back of a C-17. No matter how cold or how hot, it is the final respect we pay for our fallen brothers and sisters.

And they suck, because in that coffin is the remnant of a life, a person who's mission was finally complete here on earth and they were called home. Knowing they are safe and happy now does nothing to ease the ache inside you when you watch that procession.

I did not want to talk about it. I felt myself avoiding his questions and his eyes. I told him I hoped his year here was quiet and that he never had to go to a ramp ceremony or a memorial. They are heart wrenching, even for brothers and sisters I did not know.

Funny, I can write about it so much more easily than I can voice the words. I can't explain why. Maybe because sitting at my computer, I don't have to look in your eyes and explain to you what it feels like. Maybe because you can't see my eyes fill or my voice thicken, I can write the words far more easily than I can speak them.

For whatever reason, I don't want to talk about what it's like. In that, I am probably more like my combat veteran brothers and sisters than I am different. COL (RET) Merline Lovelace told me that most folks in her generation don't talk about Vietnam, even after years of work to remove the stigma from veterans of that war. There is a deep shame in our country for how we treated our veterans of Vietnam whereas there is a deep pride in our nation now for our veterans of this war.

It still doesn't mean I want to talk about it. I'll write about it instead, because that is my chosen release. Others may be willing to speak about it and if they do, listen. But for now, I don't wish to speak about it.

Jessica Scott

Redeployment
2009

Reentry
December 8, 2009

I SUPPOSE IT'S SUPPOSED to be a good time. I headed back to the States a few days ago. I left behind the sand and the dust and the communal living and headed home. For the first time in my life, I was the one walking across the parade field but had no family to greet me. An old friend and mentor was there to make sure I got home okay and jump start my car. It will be a few weeks before I can go get my kids, round up the animals. My husband still isn't home, either. But now I'm sitting here, alone in an empty house and feeling out of place.

I guess that for folks coming home to families and pets and a lived-in house, it is good to be home. But for me, it's strangely silent and empty. Intellectually, I know it's because the house is empty and I spent the weekend and early hours of the morning cleaning. Shopping was fun, but in an "I need this to feel normal again" way, not in an "I really want to go shopping" kind of way.

I guess in a way, my heart is kind of like my house. Empty. There is a strange disconnect inside me that I don't know how to fill. I'm hoping when my husband gets home later today that I'll feel normal again, but right now, I'm not sure. I know that life in Iraq is not real life but that life back here is strange and different, too.

I'm not sure which way is up or down. I know, intellectually, that I'm tired and I'm jet lagged and

216

I'm going through a bunch of emotional changes, but none of that helps fill what's inside me. Or rather, what's not.

So we'll see what happens as the hours turn into days. I know that time is incredibly slow. I've never had an hour take so long in my life as this last one. I'm sitting and reading a great book and the time is simply inching by. The house is clean. I have new makeup.

But it still feels like normal will only return when my house is full of kids and dogs and cats and dust bunnies the size of Chihuahuas. Maybe that is normal. Maybe that is real life.

Right now, I'm simply not sure.

What's Your Theme?
December 10, 2009

LAST NIGHT I WENT to the Austin RWA annual Christmas party. I had a fantastic time reconnecting with the women who supported me so incredibly last year while I was in Iraq. It was great and I felt like I was around a group of kindred spirits and it was one of the first times I felt normal this year.

It was literally like taking a deep breath and letting go of some of the tension I've held on to since I've been back. It was an oasis of normalcy that I desperately needed.

It was great, talking about writing and books. I loved it. But I got a question thrown at me that I was not prepared for.

What's your theme?

I pretty much stopped and really had to think about it. My books are all military in nature, but military, by itself, is not a theme. It's a topic. Themes are the something deeper, beneath the narrative and are much more universal than any story can be.

I honestly couldn't answer for a moment. I thought about Shane's story, War's Darkest Fear. He did nothing wrong, but he felt like he had. I thought about Lucas's story, Resurrection. Lucas believes in the mission but when he has to make a choice about the mission or his life, the consequences are more than he bargained for. I thought about Tracy and Sean in War's Darkest Loss. Sean had never forgiven himself for his actions and Tracy has to figure out if she can.

There are other books I've written but ultimately, looking across my body of work, the constant theme is redemption. Shane has to forgive himself for being wounded and give himself permission to live again. In Resurrection, Lucas has to atone for making the wrong choice. In Loss, Sean has to prove that he's a better man than the boy Tracy once knew.

Redemption is a theme that I've been dealing with a lot in my work and I didn't even know it. Balancing redemption is vengeance. What happens when good men and women allow vengeance to dictate their actions? I'm not certain where these themes have risen from within me, but I do know that they run through my work.

So thank you, Chris, for asking me that question. It was a tough one to answer, but I think I've figured it out.

I Am Not Anonymous
December 11, 2009

I'VE DEVELOPED A LOW tolerance for a lot of things since I've been back from Iraq, but something completely trivial is working my nerves.

People all across the country respect and admire soldiers and thank us for our service. While we're just doing our jobs like everyone else, it's still nice for people to recognize just by saying thank you that we do something just a little out of the ordinary. It's a small thing, but it really means a lot.

Except, if you live in a military town, the rule is not "thank you for your service," but "familiarity breeds contempt." So when a civilian walks by at 0758, refusing to make eye contact with me as I stand outside your office and refusing to open the door to even allow me and the three other soldiers inside where it was warm, remember that without us, you wouldn't have a job.

I know that sounds bitchy and it is. My patience, like I've pointed out, is really low these days. But these women were completely engrossed in their conversation and were literally trying to pretend that there weren't four of us outside, freezing our asses off. They couldn't even be bothered to open the door and let us in. They didn't even have to serve us before they opened, but a little common courtesy would have been nice. Especially considering it was 32 degrees.

Same thing happened at a local restaurant. This place was a chain and my hubby and I thought having a sit down breakfast would be nice. We waited, patiently. The restaurant was half empty but still, no one was coming to seat us. Then, when the hostess finally did start seating folks, she seated another couple first.

We left, neither of us having the patience to deal with such a lack of basic manners and basic customer service.

I know this sounds like I'm being petty and small and maybe I am. Maybe in a couple weeks, I'll look back on this post and wonder what the hell I was thinking. And please recognize, this is not an indictment of the whole town, but of certain people in it who refuse to recognize that soldiers are people, not just numbers.

But right now, the rudeness and the refusal by some of the people in the town and on the base I call home to recognize that soldiers are not just a uniform but a person is disconcerting.

Jessica Scott
Nothing is Trivial
December 12, 2009

I'VE BEEN HOME A few days now. I've been busy. Aside from the dead lizard in the bathroom, which I really enjoyed, I've been going nonstop.

Cleaning the house and getting things back to normal in my home is nearly a full time job. But I did take time for me, because as soon as I get the kids back, I no longer have me time. So I went and spent some time at Bobbi Brown and at The Loft and spent some time trying to learn how to be a girl again.

But here's the problem. I've been a soldier all year long. That's been who I am. Aside from the folks I interact with in the online writing community, I've been around soldiers and that's it.

It was easier.

I very nearly lost my temper today at a girl who was doing her best to cut my hair but despite her efforts was pretty much giving me a hatchet job. You'd think I would be a little more easy-going about this, seeing how my hair has had a single style for the entire year. But as the length got shorter and shorter and the sides more and more uneven, I felt this tiny knot of anger growing inside me. She was trying but the harder she tried the worse it got and the bigger the knot grew.

Thankfully a more experienced hair-stylist stepped in and salvaged it so I'm not bald.

But really? I was getting violently angry over. A HAIR

221

CUT.

WTF? This is something so beyond petty and inconsequential, I'm ashamed to even be writing about it. Everyone who knows me knows I've got a temper but as I've gotten older, I've strived to keep it more in check. This year has been more challenging and I'll admit, I let it fly more often than I checked it.

But if I'm losing my temper (which I did not, thankfully. I paid and left without comment) about something so absolutely stupid as a bad haircut, how on earth am I going to handle my kids? I mean, they're babies. They're not used to me and I'm not used to them.

So how am I going to handle this?

I'll tell you, this is the most apprehensive I've been in a long time.

This isn't a two-week stint of R&R. This is it. I'm Mommy, full time, starting in less than a week, and there's no one to take the load off for me and my husband. We're both coming back this time, not him with me adjusting to him coming home.

It's going to be an interesting journey, that's for sure.

Returning Home: Status Report
December 15, 2009

THINGS ARE SETTLING BACK in. I've been home for a week now and I'm starting to feel normal. The irritation that I feel over little things is subsiding and I'm getting back into my current WIP. I nailed twenty pages on it this weekend and I'm just starting to get back into the groove of it.

I've also had an encouraging couple of emails from prospective agents. The agents who currently have my full manuscript are ones I'd love to work with, so if I have a choice, it's going to be a hard one to make. I won't make an on-the-spot decision, but having been in one agent/author relationship, I think I have a better idea as to what I'm looking for.

In other news, I've rediscovered how to burn food and that my domestic abilities are still sorely lacking. There was no magical hit this past year that miraculously turned me into a Martha Stewart protégé. No, I still burned the first round of blueberry muffins; however, the second round (that did not come from a box) were a huge hit with my other half (trust me, this is a bigger milestone than you might think).

The biggest news this week is that on Friday, I get full swing back into Mommy mode. No more phone calls with the kiddos, I get full-blown hugs, along with peed-on pants, dirty faces, and attitude. It's going to be an adjustment, I know this, but one thing I am hoping for is a better perspective on things with them now that I'm home. I'm implementing a rule on myself: no email, no phone calls, no distractions while the kids are home from school. The few precious hours I have with them each night are going to be sacred mommy-and-kiddo time.

I personally think I'm going to go insane inside of a week. It will be a race between my mom and I as to who gets there first: me from inheriting my children back or her from the silence in her house from no children.

Either way it rolls, life is going to be an adjustment over the next few months. They say it takes ninety days for things to fully settle in. Well, in ninety days, my husband might be moving to Fort Bragg without us, with me and the kids to follow this summer. That will be an adjustment, but having gone through two deployments at home with him gone, I know I'll be just fine. Busy. But fine.

So that's the latest from the home front. With any kind of luck, I've got a new normal, just in time for that normal to be replaced, once more, by chaos. I'll live. I always do.

I Am Not One of the Guys
December 20, 2009

THE NEWS THIS WEEK was that female veterans have a hard time feeling like they're part of the team once they get back. An article ran in the Associated Press that commented that no one buys the gals a beer in the bar and they're not invited out to the bar with the families because the wives of their buddies downrange might not approve.

I can relate and in a sense, I understand. I was at a car dealership this weekend and the manager was talking to my husband about being in Iraq. I felt sidelined by the fact that the manager never once asked if I'd been there, too. He simply assumed I was a spouse and I felt like I'd be going "ooh ooh me, too, I was there, too," if I'd spoken up. It was awkward for me but at the same time, had I not read the AP article, I might not have been even thinking about it.

As a female soldier, I've always been on the outside looking in. The males in every unit I've been a part of have seen a female first, a soldier second, much like they see a black female first or a Hispanic male first. I've accepted that is simply part of being a woman in the military. I've also accepted another dirty little secret: the wives at home always seem to suspect the female soldiers in their husbands' units of trying to sleep with their husbands. Their fear is not unfounded. I get to see what some of their husbands do during the deployments and when they're TDY. Some of their husbands are not faithful and that is a disappointment to me.

They are not cheating on their wives with me, but that doesn't matter because I am simply The Other to the wives at home. I'm a woman who is not them who spends time with their husbands. So I understand the awkwardness that some of the guys have in introducing their teams. I can't smile too much when I meet the wives or else I'm suspected. I can't be too standoffish because then I'm hiding something. It's a precarious balance, one that means that when I get home, I've lost the buddies I've hung out with all year, BS-ing with them in the TOC or in the smoke area.

That means that when we come home, I'm on my own. I can't seek out the friends I had downrange without causing suspicion and rumor and the last thing anyone needs is rumor and innuendo. Coming home is hard enough without adding jealousy into the mix.

People can't help what they see. When they see a female, the mental association is not with being a soldier in our society, just like when folks see a lieutenant, they don't expect to see someone with experience. I am what people see, at least until they get to know me. I cannot change their expectations of me in that first glance but I can change it once they get to know me.

I feel like I'm doing a "me, too" thing when I correct people if they leave me out. Invariably, they are surprised that I'm in the Army because "I don't look like I'm in the Army." I'm not sure exactly what that means, but it's irrelevant. I am in the Army. I am a combat veteran. And when they shake my husband's hand and say "welcome home," I feel the lack of recognition.

Maybe I shouldn't. Maybe I should just accept it as what it is. But it still hurts.

And it still feels wrong, for me and the thousands of women who've served with distinction just like our brothers.

NOW I Am Home
December 20, 2009

I'VE BEEN TREADING WATER for the last two weeks. Two nights ago, I walked into my mother's home to cries of "Mommy, Mommy." I held my daughters in my arms and I was finally home. The piece of me that was missing is now filled. I am no longer just Jessie, just a soldier, just a writer. I'm Mommy once more, with all that entails.

And I couldn't be happier. I'm exhausted, look like hell, (remember that crappy haircut? Yeah, I've had no time to take care of it), but couldn't be happier. I've had no desire to write but that's only temporary. For now, my job is Mommy. My littlest one likes to tell me "you're the best parents in the whole wide world," even after we've left them for the entire year.

They're clingy. We cannot leave them alone and have no desire to. They fight in the car more. We made it exactly five minutes on a road trip to town before my hubby was ready to pull his hair out from the arguments and I was cracking up because, despite the time lapse, I'm still able to tune them out. Of course, he went and bought DVD players for the coming road trip to Texas.

I've done arts and crafts and gone sledding and slept in a chair holding both of them. My youngest is so far out of pull-ups, my oldest could pass for a third grader with her more mature short hair cut (I swear to God, if I catch her with scissors again...).

I've already started counting to three to overcome my three year old's selective hearing.

There's no better feeling than holding my daughters as they snuggle up. They've changed incredibly but then again, so have I. This is what's really important. The time with my kiddos. I'll never get this year back but I still have today to make a difference and let them know how much I loved them and missed them. I'll never let the opportunity pass by.

More Books by Jessica Scott

Thank you for Reading!

Thank you to the readers who emailed me while I was deployed. I hope you enjoyed learning about my Iraq experience.

Want to know when my next book is available or special sales? Signed up for my newsletter at www.jessicascott.net

You've just read the second book of my nonfiction series The Journey Home. If you'd like to read more, please check out **To Iraq & Back: On War and Writing.**

If you'd like to read my novels about soldiers coming home from war, please pick up my Coming Home series. It starts with **Because of You.** The series continues in **I'll Be Home For Christmas, Anything For You, Back to You, Until There Was You, All for You, and It's Always Been You.**

All I Want For Christmas is You: A Coming Home Novella will be available on November 11, 2014.

.

JESSICA SCOTT

THE LONG WAY HOME

AUTHOR OF TO IRAQ AND BACK

My name is Jessica Scott. I am a soldier. I am a mother. I am a wife.

In 2009, Army second lieutenant Jessica Scott deployed to Iraq as part of Operation Iraqi Freedom and Operation New Dawn. She thought deploying was the hardest thing she'd ever do.

She was wrong.

This is the story of a mother coming home from war and learning to be a mom again. This is the story of a lieutenant making the grade and becoming a company commander. This is the journey of a writer persevering through a hundred rejections. This is the story of a soldier learning to be a woman again. This is the story of a wife waiting for the end of a war.

This is the journey as it happened, without commentary.

This is her blog. There are many blogs from the Iraq war, but this one is hers.

About the Author

Jessica Scott is a career Army officer, mother of two daughters, three cats, and three dogs, wife to a career NCO, and wrangler of all things stuffed and fluffy. She is a terrible cook and even worse housekeeper, but she's a pretty good shot with her assigned weapon and someone liked some of the stuff she wrote. Somehow, her children are pretty well-adjusted and her husband still loves her, despite burned water and a messy house. No ZhuZhu Pets were harmed in the writing of this book.

Photo: Courtesy of Buzz Covington Photography

Made in the USA
Middletown, DE
19 September 2016